An Array of Challenges
Test Your SAS® Skills

ROBERT VIRGILE

The correct bibliographic citation for this manual is as follows: Virgile, Robert, *An Array of Challenges—Test Your SAS® Skills*, Cary, NC:, SAS Institute Inc., 1996. 174 pp.

An Array of Challenges–Test Your SAS® Skills

Copyright © 1996 by SAS Institute Inc., Cary, NC, USA.

ISBN 1-55544-806-2

SAS Institute Inc., SAS Campus Drive, Cary, North Carolina 27513.

1st printing, July 1996

The SAS® System is an integrated system of software providing complete control over data access, management, analysis, and presentation. Base SAS software is the foundation of the SAS System. Products within the SAS System include SAS/ACCESS®, SAS/AF®, SAS/ASSIST®, SAS/BUDGET™, SAS/CALC®, SAS/CONNECT®, SAS/CPE®, SAS/DMI®, SAS/EIS®, SAS/ENGLISH®, SAS/ETS®, SAS/FINANCE™, SAS/FSP®, SAS/GRAPH®, SAS/IMAGE®, SAS/IML®, SAS/IMS-DL/I®, SAS/INSIGHT®, SAS/LAB®, SAS/NVISION®, SAS/OR®, SAS/PH-Clinical®, SAS/QC®, SAS/REPLAY-CICS®, SAS/SESSION®, SAS/SHARE®, SAS/SPECTRAVIEW®, SAS/STAT®, SAS/TOOLKIT®, SAS/TRADER®, SAS/TUTOR®, SAS/DB2™, SAS/GEO™, SAS/GIS™, SAS/PH-Kinetics™, SAS/SHARE*NET™, and SAS/SQL-DS™ software. Other SAS Institute products are SYSTEM 2000® Data Management Software, with basic SYSTEM 2000, CREATE™, Multi-User™, QueX™, Screen Writer™, and CICS interface software; InfoTap® software; NeoVisuals® software; JMP®, JMP IN®, and JMP Serve® software; SAS/RTERM® software; and the SAS/C® Compiler and the SAS/CX® Compiler; Video Reality™ software; VisualSpace® software; and Emulus® software. MultiVendor Architecture™ and MVA™ are trademarks of SAS Institute Inc. SAS Institute also offers SAS Consulting®, SAS Video Productions®, Ambassador Select®, and On-Site Ambassador℠ services. Authorline®, Books by Users℠, The Encore Series™, *JMPer Cable®*, *Observations®*, *SAS Communications®*, *SAS Training®*, *SAS Views®*, the SASware Ballot®, and SelecText™ documentation are published by SAS Institute Inc. The SAS Video Productions logo and the Books by Users SAS Institute's Author Service logo are registered service marks and the Helplus logo, the SelecText logo, the SAS Online Samples logo, the Video Reality logo, the Quality Partner logo, and The Encore Series logo are trademarks of SAS Institute Inc. All trademarks above are registered trademarks or trademarks of SAS Institute Inc. in the USA and other countries. ® indicates USA registration.

The Institute is a private company devoted to the support and further development of its software and related services.

Other brand and product names are registered trademarks or trademarks of their respective companies.

SAS Institute does not assume responsibility for the accuracy of any material presented in this book.

CONTENTS

ACKNOWLEDGMENTS

I could not have done this by myself!

Special thanks are due to people who, over the years, have suggested possible topics for programming problems. You may or may not see your suggestions appear in print, but you always started me thinking along avenues I might never have otherwise pursued. Special thanks go to Ron Cody, Paul Grant, Karin LaPann, William MacHose, Yevgenia Mackiernan, David Parizer, Clint Rickards, and Ian Whitlock. I only hope that I haven't omitted anyone who deserves to be on this list.

The technical reviewers, editors, and production staff at SAS Institute made many excellent suggestions. Because of their work, this is undoubtedly a better book than I would have written on my own. Any errors which remain are my doing.

Finally, thanks go to my wife Paula just for being herself. No matter how clever I think I have been, she is a constant reminder that there are many important parts to life besides programming.

INTRODUCTION

The idea for this book grew out of problem-solving contests presented at NESUG and SUGI conferences. Many conference attendees commented on how much they enjoyed and learned from the contests. This book contains problems presented at previous conferences as well as a few new problems.

This book serves as a yardstick, a way of measuring your skills compared to top programmers across the country. Because many programmers with diverse skill levels have participated in problem-solving contests, I know from experience what kinds of problems a top flight programmer can solve.

Most of the skills tested here involve fundamental concepts that are necessary for you to program at an advanced level. For example, you'll see problems based on

- operation of DO loops

- lengths of variables

- merging data sets

- compilation vs. execution time in the DATA step.

Occasionally, less common topics work their way into the picture, such as macro language or the POINT= option on a SET statement. A few problems concern the LAG function, not because it's a common tool but because it illustrates the flow of execution of DATA step statements. All in all, though, these problems test base SAS software programming skills. No knowledge of add-on products is required.

As you judge your answers, award yourself partial credit liberally. This is the sort of scale I used for judging the contests:

Full Credit
Your answer must solve the problem without syntax or logic errors. Trivial oversights, such as the program not working for esoteric cases of bad data, are permitted.

3/4 Credit
Your answer would have worked, except for small syntax or logic error(s).

1/2 Credit
Your answer partially solves the problem.

1/4 Credit

Your answer used many of the proper tools, but the program just doesn't do the job.

Using this standard for grading, contest experience shows that the best programmers in the country solve 8 or 9 out of 10 problems. Use this scale as a guideline:

80% to 100% correct = Upper echelon SAS programmer

60% to 80% correct = Advanced level programmer

40% to 60% correct = Solid skills

20% to 40% correct = Areas of strength need to be broadened

Less than 20% = Treat this as a learning experience

There are just a few ground rules. Take as much time as you would like to take. Feel free to use manuals, but not computers. Finally, remember that learning is more important than having a correct answer. You gain the most by working at the problems, not skipping to the answers. Learn new programming techniques, and ingrain those you already know. To quote Theodore Roosevelt (from an address at the Sorbonne, Paris, France, April 23, 1910):

> Credit belongs to the man who really was in the arena, his face marred by dust and sweat and blood; who strives valiantly; who errs and comes short again and again, because there is no effort without error and shortcoming; but who does actually strive to do the deeds; who knows the great enthusiasms the great devotions; who spends himself in a worthy cause; who at best knows in the end the triumph of high achievement, and who at the worst, if he fails, at least fails while daring greatly, so that his place shall never be with those cold and timid souls who know neither victory nor defeat.

More than one problem illustrates common themes such as functions or determining the lengths of variables. As in real life, problems with a common theme are not grouped, but rather are spread throughout the book. An appendix categorizes problems by the programming tools and concepts used.

Some problems ask whether two programs produce identical results. "Identical" means two data sets contain the same data values, and use the same variable names. Don't worry about the internal storage order of the variables and variable attributes other than name, length, and type.

Finally, a few technical assumptions:

- If a data set or variable is mentioned, assume that it exists.

- If a BY statement is used, the data are already sorted.

- If a mentioned format cannot be found, an error message will be generated.

- If a dropped, kept, or renamed variable cannot be found, an error message will be generated.

Take note: Some problems have more than one solution! Take credit if you correctly solve a problem, whether or not you use the same methods as the sample solution. In many cases, sample solutions present more than one approach.

As a matter of style, the problems do not use RUN statements. If you would prefer, feel free to envision a RUN statement at the end of each complete DATA and PROC step.

Composing short but tough problems is more difficult than it might seem. Feel free to suggest new ones, or variations on those you see here. Please send all suggestions and comments to:

> Robert Virgile
> c/o User Publishing Program
> SAS Institute Inc.
> SAS Campus Drive
> Cary, NC 27513

Good luck!

Have fun!

I hope you learn a lot!

PART I

20 BASICS AND BUILDING BLOCKS

Problems appear in Part 1 because

1. they're easier, or

2. they serve as building blocks for more complex problems in Part 2.

Working on these problems lets you determine whether or not you are ready to attempt the more complex problems that follow. If you miss some of the answers to these problems, study the tools and programming techniques until you are comfortable with them. In that way, you'll gain many of the skills needed to attempt the more difficult problems.

As a rule, these are intermediate (not introductory) problems. The intent of this book is to build on the skills of programmers who are already using SAS software.

Each problem lists related tools and concepts. An appendix cross-references topics, so you can easily find other problems that use similar tools. To a small extent, the list of topics can guide you toward a solution. If you would rather not have any hints, cover up the bottom of the page as you read the problem. The problem titles are merely titles, not hints.

PROBLEM I

Functionally Literate

What is the final value of PACKAGE in this program?

```
DATA TEST;
PACKAGE = 'SAS';
PART1 = SUBSTR(PACKAGE,1,1);
PART2 = SUBSTR(PACKAGE,2,1);
PART3 = SUBSTR(PACKAGE,3,1);
PACKAGE = PART3 || PART2 || PART1;
```

Tools and concepts:

Functions

Lengths of variables

```
DATA TEST;
PACKAGE = 'SAS';
PART1 = SUBSTR(PACKAGE,1,1);
PART2 = SUBSTR(PACKAGE,2,1);
PART3 = SUBSTR(PACKAGE,3,1);
PACKAGE = PART3 || PART2 || PART1;
```

PACKAGE has a length of 3.

The other variables, PART1-PART3, also have a length of 3. When the SUBSTR function creates a new variable, the length assigned to that variable is the same as the length of the incoming character string.

PART1, therefore, is an "S" followed by two blanks.

PART2 is an "A" followed by two blanks.

PART3 is an "S" followed by two blanks.

The fully concatenated string is nine characters long:

        S   A   S

including two trailing blanks. When this string is assigned as the value of PACKAGE, there is only room to store the first three characters. Therefore, PACKAGE is an "S" followed by two blanks.

PROBLEM 2

First Obs Impressions

If OLD contains 100 observations, which of those get printed?

```
OPTIONS FIRSTOBS=5 OBS=20;

PROC SORT DATA=OLD OUT=NEW;
BY ID;

PROC PRINT DATA=NEW;
```

Tools and concepts:

Global options

```
OPTIONS FIRSTOBS=5 OBS=20;

PROC SORT DATA=OLD OUT=NEW;
BY ID;

PROC PRINT DATA=NEW;
```

Both options (FIRSTOBS and OBS) remain in effect throughout the program, affecting any subsequent step that reads data. In this case, both PROC SORT and PROC PRINT are affected.

The FIRSTOBS option says that when you are reading from any source of data, begin with the 5th observation. The OBS option says when reading from any source of data, end with the 20th observation.

PROC SORT reads in observations, sorts them, and then writes them back out. Thus the effect of the options is that PROC SORT reads in only 16 observations, the 5th through 20th from OLD. Those 16 observations, in sorted order by ID, are written back out to NEW.

PROC PRINT then reads in the remaining observations, and prints them. Because of the FIRSTOBS option, PROC PRINT begins printing with the 5th observation from NEW. Thus, the printed observations are: out of observations 5 through 20 from OLD, those with the 12 highest values for ID.

PROBLEM 3

Keep Your Day Job

The author of these words quickly abandoned his dreams of becoming a writer and
became a successful programmer instead. Under what conditions, if any, would these
SAS statements execute without error?

```
DATA MEANS NOTHING; SET YOUR MIND TO THE TASK; PUT YOUR
SHOULDER TO THE WHEEL.  WITH THE PROPER RATIO OF
WORK/DESIRE -- PLUS A LITTLE LUCK -- ALL YOUR DREAMS
CAN COME TRUE.  ;
```

Tools and concepts:

Customized reporting
Variable lists

```
DATA MEANS NOTHING; SET YOUR MIND TO THE TASK; PUT YOUR
SHOULDER TO THE WHEEL.  WITH THE PROPER RATIO OF
WORK/DESIRE —— PLUS A LITTLE LUCK —— ALL YOUR DREAMS
CAN COME TRUE.  ;
```

Here are the conditions:

- The following formats must exist: WHEEL and TRUE.

- The following data sets must exist: YOUR, MIND, TO, THE, and TASK.

- The variables named in the PUT statement may or may not be contained in these data sets, subject to three restrictions:

  1. The variables THE and COME, if they exist, must be numeric.

  2. If either DESIRE or PLUS exists, both must exist.

  3. If either LUCK or ALL exists, both must exist.

For the last two pairs of variables, the order is important. The double hyphen (——) means "all variables beginning with the first and ending with the second," so the words:

```
DESIRE —— PLUS
```

denote a list of all variables beginning with DESIRE and ending with PLUS. The variables do not have to come from the same data set. However, the internal storage position of DESIRE must come before the internal storage position of PLUS for the double hyphen to be valid. Internal storage position is the same as the order in which the variables were defined. PROC CONTENTS (or the CONTENTS statement within PROC DATASETS) reveals the internal storage position as well as much more information about each variable.

If any variable in the PUT statement does not exist, the software automatically creates it. Such variables may be uninitialized (meaning they were never assigned a value), but they will "exist" in the sense that storage space in memory is reserved to hold their values. Each new uninitialized variable will be numeric in this program.

PROBLEM 4

Any Comments?

This program attempts to print the results of PROC SUMMARY. Describe any errors in these statements and how to correct them.

```
****************************;
***   COMPUTE THE AVERAGE   ***;
***   COST; PRINT RESULTS. ***;
****************************;

PROC SUMMARY DATA=SALES;
VAR COST;

PROC PRINT;
```

Tools and concepts:

Comments
PROC MEANS/PROC SUMMARY

```
***************************;
***   COMPUTE THE AVERAGE   ***;
***   COST; PRINT RESULTS. ***;
***************************;

PROC SUMMARY DATA=SALES;
VAR COST;

PROC PRINT;
```

There are two problems here:

1   There is an extra semicolon within the block of comments.

2. There is no summary data set for PROC PRINT to process.

An initial asterisk comments out a SAS statement, not an entire line. Thus the semicolon after COST (in line 3) ends a comment statement. The next statement,

```
PRINT RESULTS. ***;
```

is an invalid SAS statement.

PROC SUMMARY requires an OUTPUT statement to create an output data set. Without it, PROC PRINT can't print the results of PROC SUMMARY. (It would print the most recently created SAS data set instead.)

As an alternative, add the PRINT option, eliminating PROC PRINT:

```
PROC SUMMARY DATA=SALES PRINT;
VAR COST;
```

Retained Knowledge

The SAS System must determine the values of I and J so that the PUT statement can write them to the SAS log. What messages are written by the PUT statement, if any?

```
DATA TEST;
DO I = 1 TO 3;
    OUTPUT;
END;

DATA _NULL_;
PUT I= J=;
SET TEST;
RETAIN J 25;
J = I;
```

Tools and concepts:

Customized reporting
DATA step flow
RETAIN statement/Sum statement

```
DATA TEST;
DO I = 1 TO 3;
   OUTPUT;
END;

DATA _NULL_;
PUT I= J=;
SET TEST;
RETAIN J 25;
J = I;
```

TEST contains three observations, with I taking on the values 1 through 3. Since the DATA step does not read from any external source of data, the DATA step ends after executing the DO loop. This technique comes in handy when creating test data sets. For example, to test a program against a data set containing 5000 observations and 100 numeric variables, you don't need to find such a data set. Instead, you can create one easily:

```
DATA TEST;
DO VAR1 = 1 TO 5000;
   OUTPUT;
END;
RETAIN VAR2-VAR100 0;
```

When a PUT statement uses an equal sign (I= J=), it writes the variable names, an equal sign, and the values. In the original program, the RETAIN statement assigns J a value of 25 initially, during the compilation phase. Since I is read from a SAS data set, it is retained also. That part is automatic: any variable read from a SAS data set is automatically retained. So the messages are

```
I=.  J=25
I=1  J=1
I=2  J=2
I=3  J=3
```

The program writes four sets of messages, not three. AFTER the fourth set of messages get written, the SET statement fails because there are no more observations left to read from the data set TEST. That is the normal ending for the DATA step.

PROBLEM 6

The I's Have It

What is the final value of I?

```
DO I = 1 TO 5;
    I = 3 * I;
END;
```

Tools and concepts:

DO loops

```
DO I = 1 TO 5;
    I = 3 * I;
END;
```

Each time the program reaches the END statement, it goes through these steps:

1. Increase I by 1.

2. Compare I to the upper limit of 5. If I is greater than 5, end the loop.

Complicating the process is the fact that statements within the DO loop can change the value of I. In this program, then, the steps are

1. At the DO statement, give I an initial value of 1. (I=1)

2. At the assignment statement, multiply I by 3. (I=3)

3. At the END statement, increase I by 1. (I=4)

4. Since I is still less than or equal to 5 (the outer bound of the loop), go through the loop again.

5. At the assignment statement, multiply I by 3. (I=12)

6. At the END statement, increase I by 1. (I=13)

7. Since 13 is greater than 5, the loop now ends.

The final value of I is 13.

PROBLEM 7

Finding True Love

Which combination(s) produce(s) TRUE LOVE?

```
IF ('TED' <  'ALICE'  <  'BOB'  <  'CAROL')
THEN PUT 'TRUE LOVE';


IF ('TED' < ('ALICE'  <  'BOB') <  'CAROL')
THEN PUT 'TRUE LOVE';


IF ('TED' <  'ALICE') < ('BOB'  <  'CAROL')
THEN PUT 'TRUE LOVE';
```

Tools and concepts:

Logical comparisons

```
IF ('TED' <  'ALICE'  <  'BOB'  <  'CAROL')
THEN PUT 'TRUE LOVE';

IF ('TED' < ('ALICE'  <  'BOB') <  'CAROL')
THEN PUT 'TRUE LOVE';

IF ('TED' <  'ALICE') < ('BOB'  <  'CAROL')
THEN PUT 'TRUE LOVE';
```

Only the last combination produces "TRUE LOVE".

Two considerations apply here:

1. When making a series of comparisons, all comparisons must be true for the entire expression to be true.

2. When a comparison is evaluated, it gets replaced with a 1 (if true) or a 0 (if false).

The first series of comparisons is false. The SAS System compares "TED" to "ALICE" by comparing the first letter of each. Since "T" is greater than "A," the comparison is false. Therefore, the entire series of comparisons is false.

The second series of comparisons is also false. Because of the parentheses, the first comparison made is "ALICE" vs. "BOB". Since the comparison is true, it gets replaced with the numeric value 1, and the software now evaluates:

```
'TED' < 1 < 'CAROL'
```

As you might expect, the comparison is false. In attempting to make the comparisons, the software tries to convert "TED" and "CAROL" to numeric values and cannot make the conversion.

Parentheses govern the final series of comparisons. The software first compares "TED" to "ALICE". Since the comparison is false, it gets replaced with a 0:

```
(0 < ('BOB' < 'CAROL'))
```

Next, the software compares "BOB" to "CAROL". Since the comparison is true, it gets replaced with a 1. Since $0 < 1$, the entire expression is now true.

Functioning Smoothly

This program creates a frequency table based on the first four characters of PARTNO. Make the program more efficient by eliminating the SUBSTR function. What other major efficiencies could you introduce?

```
DATA JUSTFOUR;
SET PARTS;
PART4 = SUBSTR(PARTNO,1,4);

PROC FREQ DATA=JUSTFOUR;
TABLES PART4;
```

Tools and concepts:

    Formats
    Functions
    PROC FREQ

```
DATA JUSTFOUR;
SET PARTS;
PART4 = SUBSTR(PARTNO,1,4);

PROC FREQ DATA=JUSTFOUR;
TABLES PART4;
```

Within the DATA step, PART4 is longer than it needs to be. When the SUBSTR function creates a new variable, the length assigned is the same as the length of the incoming character string. Assigning PART4 a length of 4 is easy with a LENGTH statement. However, once a LENGTH statement is used, SUBSTR is no longer needed:

```
LENGTH PART4 $ 4;
PART4 = PARTNO;
```

Now PART4 has enough room to hold the first four characters only from PARTNO without needing a function.

Even more efficient is to eliminate the DATA step entirely.

```
PROC FREQ DATA=PARTS;
TABLES PARTNO;
FORMAT PARTNO $4.;
```

The FORMAT statement in PROC FREQ groups PARTNO according to the first four characters. There is no need for a new data set or a new variable.

PROBLEM 9

Before the Execution

TEST1 and TEST2 each hold 1 observation and 2 variables. What are the lengths and values of A and B in the two data sets?

```
DATA TEST1;
LENGTH A 3 B $ 2;
RETAIN _NUMERIC_ 0 _CHARACTER_ 'ABC';

DATA TEST2;
RETAIN _NUMERIC_ 0 _CHARACTER_ 'ABC';
LENGTH A 3 B $ 2;
```

Tools and concepts:

DATA step flow
Lengths of variables
Variable lists

```
DATA TEST1;
LENGTH A 3 B $ 2;
RETAIN _NUMERIC_ 0 _CHARACTER_ 'ABC';

DATA TEST2;
RETAIN _NUMERIC_ 0 _CHARACTER_ 'ABC';
LENGTH A 3 B $ 2;
```

Both statements, LENGTH and RETAIN, have an effect as the DATA step statements get compiled. (RETAIN has an additional effect as the DATA step executes.) The statements get compiled in order, with the order causing different outcomes in the two DATA steps.

In TEST1, B gets assigned a length of 2. The RETAIN statement then assigns an initial value of ABC to all character variables. Since the variable B has a length of 2, it only has room to store the first two characters, AB.

In TEST2, no numeric variables exist when the RETAIN statement executes (outside of automatic variables such as _N_ and _ERROR_). The meaning of _NUMERIC_ is "all numeric variables that currently exist in the Program Data Vector" not "all numeric variables that get created by later programming statements." So A and B remain unaffected by the RETAIN statement. Neither has an initial value, and neither will be retained.

To see the final results, use PROC CONTENTS to display the lengths and PROC PRINT to display the data values:

Data set	Variable	Value	Length
TEST1	A	0	3
	B	AB	$2
TEST2	A	.	3
	B		$2

Multiplying Like Rabbits

In PETSTORE, each observation represents one pet store that can stock up to 80 pets. GOATS should contain one observation for each pet store with a goat, and RABBITS should contain one observation for each pet store with a rabbit. However, pet stores that stocked multiple goats or rabbits were output too many times. Come up with a practical solution.

```
DATA GOATS RABBITS;
SET PETSTORE;
ARRAY PETS {80} PET1-PET80;
DO I = 1 TO 80;
    IF PETS{I} = 'GOAT' THEN OUTPUT GOATS;
    ELSE IF PETS{I} = 'RABBIT' THEN OUTPUT RABBITS;
END;
```

Tools and concepts:

Arrays
DO loops
OUTPUT statement

The problem: More than one of the 80 variables may contain the word GOAT or RAB-BIT. The store gets output once per match, not once per store. Any solution must track whether the observation has already been output so that it can be output only once per data set. Either counting or flagging will accomplish the necessary tracking. Here is a counting example:

```
G=0;
R=0;
DO I = 1 TO 80;
   IF PETS{I} = 'GOAT' THEN DO;
      IF G = 0 THEN OUTPUT GOATS;
      G + 1;
   END;
   ELSE IF PETS{I} = 'RABBIT' THEN DO;
      IF R = 0 THEN OUTPUT RABBITS;
      R + 1;
   END;
END;
```

Here is a flagging example:

```
G='N';
R='N';
DO I = 1 TO 80;
   IF PETS{I} = 'GOAT' THEN DO;
      IF G = 'N' THEN OUTPUT GOATS;
      G = 'Y';
   END;
   ELSE IF PETS{I} = 'RABBIT' THEN DO;
      IF R = 'N' THEN OUTPUT RABBITS;
      R = 'Y';
   END;
END;
```

Although not necessary for producing a correct solution, consider ending the DO loop as early as possible. The following statements could be added as the last statement of the outer DO loops:

```
IF G > 0 AND R > 0 THEN RETURN;

IF G = 'Y' AND R = 'Y' THEN RETURN;
```

The RETURN statement returns to the DATA statement, outputting the observation.

What if the objective were slightly different? Instead of outputting the observation in its current form, finish the DO loop as early as possible and continue processing subsequent DATA step statements. These statements would do the trick:

```
IF G > 0 AND R > 0 THEN LEAVE /* OR I = 80 */;

IF G = 'Y' AND R = 'Y' THEN LEAVE /* OR I = 80*/;
```

PROBLEM II

Don't Lag Behind

Under what circumstances, if any, will these programs produce identical results?

```
DATA NEW;                        DATA NEW;
SET OLD (KEEP=X);                Y = X;
Y = LAG(X);                      SET OLD (KEEP=X);
```

Tools and concepts:

DATA step flow

Functions

RETAIN statement/Sum statement

```
DATA NEW;                        DATA NEW;
SET OLD (KEEP=X);                Y = X;
Y = LAG(X);                      SET OLD (KEEP=X);
```

The results are identical as long as X is numeric.

If X were character, the second program would generate an error. The assignment statement would create two new variables, X and Y. By default those variables would be numeric. The SET statement would then attempt to define X as a character variable. Since the same variable cannot be defined as both character and numeric, the software would generate an error message.

More importantly, why should the results be identical when X is numeric? These two factors produce the result:

1. The LAG function retrieves the value of X from the last time the function executed. Usually, this means the value of X from the previous observation.

2. Every variable read from a SAS data set (using a SET, MERGE, or UPDATE statement) is automatically retained.

With the first program, then, Y is missing on the first observation. On every other observation, Y is the value of X from the previous observation.

With the second program, Y will also be missing on the first observation. The assignment statement executes before the SET statement, so X is missing at that time. Next, the SET statement executes, reading in the first value for X, and generating the same result as the first program for observation 1. As the DATA step continues to execute, X is retained. Therefore, the assignment statement next gives Y the value of X on the first observation. The SET statement executes, replacing X with the value on the second observation, generating the same result as the first program: on observation 2, the value of Y is the same as the value of X on the first observation.

These programs illustrate an important principle necessary to program at an advanced level. The SET statement is much more than a label indicating where the data will be coming from. It is an executable statement which reads in a single observation. It really means "go out to data set OLD and retrieve the next observation into the Program Data Vector." The software tracks which observations have been read in already and "knows" which observation is next.

Pork Barrel Legislation

The following program counts the number of pork barrel observations in a SAS data set. When tested, the program worked just fine. However, the next day, when the program ran against a different SAS data set, no report was generated. There were no error messages either day.

1. What happened?

2. What other possibilities would exist if the WHERE statement were an IF statement instead?

```
DATA _NULL_;
SET LAWS END=EOF;
WHERE STATUS = 'BARREL' AND TYPE = 'PORK';
TOTAL + 1;
IF EOF THEN PUT //
    'TOTAL NUMBER OF PORK BARREL LAWS IS ' TOTAL;
```

Tools and concepts:

DATA step flow
Detecting end-of-file
Subsetting IF/DELETE
WHERE statement

The program produces no report when no observations meet the WHERE conditions. The SET statement then has no data to read. As a result, the last statement, searching for end-of-file, never gets executed. The DATA step ends before executing that statement.

When using a subsetting IF instead of WHERE, the last observation only is the one that matters. With a subsetting IF, the program goes through a different process for each observation:

1. The SET statement reads in an observation.

2. The subsetting IF examines the observation, possibly deleting it.

3. If the observation has not been deleted, it gets processed against the remaining statements.

If the final observation gets deleted by the subsetting IF, the check for end-of-file never gets executed for that observation. Next, the SET statement fails because it runs out of observations to read; therefore, the DATA step ends.

The solution in either case is to check for end-of-file before the SET statement:

```
DATA _NULL_;
IF EOF THEN PUT //
    'TOTAL NUMBER OF PORK BARREL LAWS IS ' TOTAL;
SET LAWS END=EOF;
WHERE STATUS = 'BARREL' AND TYPE = 'PORK';
*IF   STATUS = 'BARREL' AND TYPE = 'PORK';
TOTAL + 1;
```

WHERE looks ahead and sets EOF to 1 when no additional observations meet the WHERE conditions. If zero observations meet the WHERE conditions, EOF is originally 1. In any case, the program checks for end-of-file and finds EOF=1 just before the SET statement fails.

IF may or may not delete the last observation. Either way, the program returns to the DATA statement and continues executing. Next, the software checks EOF and generates a report. Finally, the SET statement fails because there are no more observations to read.

Do Bring Sunscreen

Sketch the contents of FLORIDA.

```
DATA FLORIDA;
DO TOURISTS = 1 TO 3;
   DO CITY = 'TAMPA', 'MIAMI', 'ORLANDO';
      OUTPUT;
   END;
END;
IF TOURISTS = 3;
```

DO loops
Lengths of variables
OUTPUT statement
Subsetting IF/DELETE

CITY has a length of 5, since the program first mentions CITY by setting it equal to TAMPA (5 characters long).

The OUTPUT statement has a two-fold meaning. First, it means "right here and now, without doing any further work, output the observation." Second, it means "output only when the OUTPUT statement executes." No longer will the program output an observation merely because it hits the bottom of the DATA step. Consider this DATA step as an example:

```
DATA NEW;
SET OLD;
NEWVAR1 = 5;
OUTPUT;
NEWVAR2 = 5;
```

The data set NEW contains both NEWVAR1 and NEWVAR2, because both are mentioned in the programming statements. However, NEWVAR2 always has a missing value because the OUTPUT statement executes before the assignment statement. In addition, NEW contains the same number of observations as OLD. No observations get output after executing NEWVAR2=5.

In the original program above, the OUTPUT statement executes for each of 9 combinations of values for TOURISTS and CITY. Later, the program hits the subsetting IF statement. Therefore, the subsetting IF has no effect on the outcome. The final data set contains nine observations:

TOURISTS	CITY
1	TAMPA
1	MIAMI
1	ORLAN
2	TAMPA
2	MIAMI
2	ORLAN
3	TAMPA
3	MIAMI
3	ORLAN

PROBLEM 14

Summary Judgment

What is the final value of TOTAL?

```
DATA _NULL_;
ARRAY AMOUNTS {20} VAR1-VAR20;
DO I = 50 TO 98 BY 5;
    AMOUNTS{I/5} = I;
END;
TOTAL = SUM(VAR18-VAR20);
```

Tools and concepts:

Arrays
DO loops
Functions

```
DATA _NULL_;
ARRAY AMOUNTS {20} VAR1-VAR20;
DO I = 50 TO 98 BY 5;
   AMOUNTS{I/5} = I;
END;
TOTAL = SUM(VAR18-VAR20);
```

The DO loop executes 10 times, for values of I from 50 through 95. At the end of the tenth execution of the DO loop, I gets increased by 5 one more time, from 95 to 100. Because 100 is greater than 98 (the upper bound of the loop), the loop ends at that point.

This loop, therefore, assigns values to 10 elements of the array: VAR10 through VAR19. The first time through the loop: I=50 and I/5=10; therefore, the loop changes the tenth element, VAR10, to 50. The last time through the loop: I=95 and I/5=19; therefore, the loop changes the nineteenth element, VAR19, to 95. So when the loop is over, VAR20 is missing, VAR19 is 95, and VAR18 is 90.

The SUM function adds numbers, disregarding missing values. The following SUM function adds four arguments:

```
SUM(5, SALES, VAR1-VAR3, OF VAR5-VAR8)
```

The arguments are

1. the numeric value 5

2. the value of the variable SALES

3. VAR1 minus VAR3

4. the variables VAR5 through VAR8.

The keyword OF differentiates between subtraction and a list of variable names. In the original problem, the SUM function has only one argument: VAR18 minus VAR20. Since VAR20 is missing, the difference is also missing and TOTAL is assigned a missing value. (When every argument to the SUM function is missing, the result is a missing value, not 0.)

In Trouble

These programs attempted to evaluate the efficiency of the IN operator. What happened?

```
DATA _NULL_;                    DATA _NULL_;
TEAM = 'YANKEES';               TEAM = 'YANKEES';
DO I = 1 TO 100000;             DO I = 1 TO 1000000;
    IF TEAM = 'YANKEES'             IF TEAM IN
    OR TEAM = 'TIGERS'              ('YANKEES', 'TIGERS')
    THEN DELETE;                    THEN DELETE;
END;                            END;
```

DO loops

Subsetting IF/DELETE

```
DATA _NULL_;                    DATA _NULL_;
TEAM = 'YANKEES';               TEAM = 'YANKEES';
DO I = 1 TO 100000;             DO I = 1 TO 1000000;
    IF TEAM = 'YANKEES'             IF TEAM IN
    OR TEAM = 'TIGERS'              ('YANKEES', 'TIGERS')
    THEN DELETE;                    THEN DELETE;
END;                            END;
```

The DO loops call for different numbers of iterations (100,000 versus 1,000,000); however, that's not the problem here. Neither DATA step gets that far. Consider the meaning of the DELETE statement: return to the DATA statement without outputting the current observation. When the DELETE statement executes in the programs above, the DO loop (as well as any other programming statements) is over for that observation. The test for efficiency failed because both DO loops ended prematurely, after less than one full iteration through the loop.

This style of programming is quite valuable for testing efficiency. Instead of searching for a data set with 100,000 observations, execute the statements 100,000 times with only a single observation. For example, you could modify these programs to produce a valid test (make sure both DO loops execute 100,000 times) by replacing the word DELETE with the assignment statement X=5.

An All-American Array

Improve the efficiency of this code, while still using arrays:

```
ARRAY BASEBALL {9} INNING1-INNING9;
ARRAY PERCENTS {9} P1-P9;
DO I = 1 TO 9;
   IF STATUS = 'COMPLETE' THEN PERCENTS{I} =
   BASEBALL{I} / SUM(OF INNING1-INNING9);
END;
```

Tools and concepts:

    Arrays
    DO loops
    Functions

```
ARRAY BASEBALL {9} INNING1-INNING9;
ARRAY PERCENTS {9} P1-P9;
DO I = 1 TO 9;
   IF STATUS = 'COMPLETE' THEN PERCENTS{I} =
   BASEBALL{I} / SUM(OF INNING1-INNING9);
END;
```

The inefficiencies stem from two sources. On each observation

1. The variable STATUS remains the same each time through the loop.

2. The SUM function generates the same total every time through the loop.

Both of these items should be addressed outside the DO loop. Perform them once instead of nine times per observation.

```
IF STATUS = 'COMPLETE' THEN DO;
   TOTAL = SUM(OF INNING1-INNING9);
   DO I = 1 TO 9;
      PERCENTS{I} = BASEBALL{I} / TOTAL;
   END;
END;
```

For extra credit, take advantage of the fact that multiplication runs faster than division. One last modification, then, would be the following:

```
IF STATUS = 'COMPLETE' THEN DO;
   TOTAL = 1 / SUM(OF INNING1-INNING9);
   DO I = 1 TO 9;
      PERCENTS{I} = BASEBALL{I} * TOTAL;
   END;
END;
```

All Comments Are Welcome

Describe both the error message and its cause.

```
/*****************************************
*** This is a test of using embedded  ***
*** comments, such as:                ***
***    /* Select only the males */    ***
*****************************************/

DATA MALES;
SET EVERYONE;
IF SEX = 'M'; /* Select only the males */
```

Comments

```
/*****************************************
*** This is a test of using embedded  ***
*** comments, such as:                ***
***    /* Select only the males */    ***
*****************************************/

DATA MALES;
SET EVERYONE;
IF SEX = 'M'; /* Select only the males */
```

Embedded comments are not like left-hand and right-hand parentheses. You do not have to balance each /* with a */ like you would with parentheses or quotation marks. Once the program encounters the characters /*, all the text which follows is a comment until the next */ is encountered.

This program begins with /*, the start of an embedded comment. The embedded comment ends with the */ following the word "males" on line 4. All text in between (including /* before the word "Select") is part of the comment.

Next, a SAS statement begins with an asterisk (the three asterisks at the end of line 4). This comments out the entire SAS statement, including all characters until the next semicolon is encountered. Therefore, DATA MALES is part of a comment statement.

What error messages does the SAS System generate? Both the SET and subsetting IF statements are invalid. They can only be used in a DATA step, but there is no DATA statement in this program.

Prepare to Merge

In this many-to-one merge, how many observations were accepted from the ONE data set? Modify the DATA step so it prints the number.

```
DATA COMBINED;
MERGE MANY (IN=KEEPME) ONE;
BY ID;
IF KEEPME;
```

Assume that ONE contains just one observation per ID. Some IDs may appear in one data set but not in the other.

DATA step flow
Data set options
Detecting end-of-file
MERGE statement

```
DATA COMBINED;
MERGE MANY (IN=KEEPME) ONE;
BY ID;
IF KEEPME;
```

The IN= data set option can detect matches and mismatches in a merge. Mastering the technique is mandatory for programming at an advanced level.

To determine whether an observation was read from the ONE data set, you need a second IN= variable:

```
DATA COMBINED;
MERGE MANY (IN=KEEPME) ONE (IN=FROMONE);
BY ID;
IF KEEPME;
```

To count each ID only once, you need to use BY variables:

```
DATA COMBINED;
IF EOF THEN PUT N 'OBSERVATIONS FROM ONE.';
MERGE MANY (IN=KEEPME) ONE (IN=FROMONE) END=EOF;
BY ID;
IF KEEPME;
IF FIRST.ID AND FROMONE THEN N + 1;
DROP N;
```

END= gets applied once for the entire MERGE statement, not once per incoming data set. As with Problem 12, it is important to put the check for end-of-file before the MERGE statement. Otherwise, the report would not get printed when the last ID appears in ONE but not in MANY.

Life in the Big City

This program attempted to extract all cities from states containing a large city (one million or more people). Why did it fail?

```
DATA BIGCITY;
SET USA;
BY STATE DESCENDING POP;
IF FIRST.STATE AND POP >= 1000000 THEN FLAG = '1';
RETAIN FLAG;
IF FLAG = '1';
```

Tools and concepts:
RETAIN statement/Sum statement
Subsetting IF/DELETE

```
DATA BIGCITY;
SET USA;
BY STATE DESCENDING POP;
IF FIRST.STATE AND POP >= 1000000 THEN FLAG = '1';
RETAIN FLAG;
IF FLAG = '1';
```

This program uses many correct tools:

1. On the first observation for each STATE, assign a value to FLAG, indicating whether this STATE belongs in the output data set.

2. Retain that value, so it is available on subsequent observations for that STATE.

3. Subset the observations based on the FLAG variable.

The key missing ingredient is resetting FLAG. Once FLAG is set to 1, it remains 1 for the duration of the DATA step. All subsequent observations, regardless of which STATE they belong to, get output to the BIGCITY data set.

The solution is straightforward. Assign not just values of 1, but values of 0 as well:

```
IF FIRST.STATE THEN DO;
   IF POP >= 1000000 THEN FLAG = '1';
   ELSE FLAG = '0';
END;
```

PROBLEM 20

Merging onto the Information Superhighway

The SAS data set TWO contains two variables and two observations:

KEY	FROMTWO
1	1
1	2

The SAS data set FOUR contains two variables and four observations:

KEY	FROMFOUR
1	1
1	2
1	3
1	4

After you have run the following program, what does TOGETHER contain? (List the data values, not just the number of variables and observations.)

```
DATA TOGETHER;
MERGE TWO FOUR;
BY KEY;
IF FROMFOUR = 3 THEN FROMTWO = 3;
```

Tools and concepts:

DATA step flow
MERGE statement
RETAIN statement/Sum statement

```
DATA TOGETHER;
MERGE TWO FOUR;
BY KEY;
IF FROMFOUR = 3 THEN FROMTWO = 3;
```

The final data set:

KEY	FROMTWO	FROMFOUR
1	1	1
1	2	2
1	3	3
1	3	4

The MERGE statement is more than a label indicating where the data come from. It is an instruction that says (in part):

> See if the first data source contains any more observations for the current value of KEY. If it does, read in the next observation. Then go on to the next source of data, repeating this process.

Any variable read from a SAS data set (such as FROMTWO coming from TWO) is automatically retained. In the case of the MERGE statement, the possibilities are a little more complex. When does the MERGE statement reinitialize retained variables?

1. Variables being read from any data set on the MERGE statement get reinitialized to missing whenever a new value of the BY variable(s) begins.

2. Variables being retained for other reasons, such as a RETAIN statement or a Sum statement, never get reinitialized except by brute force. The program must contain an assignment statement that specifically changes these variables in order for them to change.

In the original program, all three variables are initially missing. The program then begins to read in data from the two sources using these steps:

Steps	Value Stored in Memory		
	KEY	FROMTWO	FROMFOUR
Determine first KEY	1		
Read from TWO	1	1	
Read from FOUR	1	1	1
IF/THEN statement	1	1	1 → Output
More data for KEY=1?*	1	1	1
Read from TWO	1	2	1
Read from FOUR	1	2	2
IF/THEN Statement	1	2	2 → Output
More data for KEY=1?*	1	2	2
Read from FOUR	1	2	3
IF/THEN Statement	1	3	3 → Output
More data for KEY=1?*	1	3	3
Read from FOUR	1	3	4
IF/THEN Statement	1	3	4 → Output

*At these points, if neither data set had contained additional observations for KEY=1, the SAS System would have reinitialized FROMONE and FROMTWO to missing, and would have searched the data sets to find the next value of KEY

Once a data value has been read from TWO, it never gets reread. The last value of FROMTWO is retained in memory, as subsequent observations are read from FOUR. Once FROMTWO runs out of observations for KEY=1, the only way FROMTWO changes is by either executing an assignment statement changing FROMTWO or by beginning to process a new value for KEY. While the example used in this problem contains a many-to-many merge, the same lesson applies in a many-to-one merge. Be very careful about changing a variable that was read from the "one" data set of a many-to-one merge. For example, consider these two data sets:

1. POWER contains one observation per state, where the variable POWER is the principal source of power for that state.

2. CITIES contains one observation per city.

These are the original data, for one state:

```
<<<<POWER>>>>              <<<<<<<<<CITIES>>>>>>>>>
STATE    POWER             STATE    CITY


PA       OIL               PA       HARRISBURG
                           PA       PHILADELPHIA
                           PA       PITTSBURGH
                           PA       THREE MILE ISLAND
                           PA       WILKES-BARRE
                           PA       WILLIAMSPORT
```

Both data sets contain the variable STATE. A program attempts to merge by STATE, to add POWER to each CITIES observation.

```
PROC SORT DATA=CITIES;
BY STATE;

PROC SORT DATA=POWER;
BY STATE;

DATA COMBINED;
MERGE CITIES (IN=KEEPME) POWER;
BY STATE;
IF KEEPME;
```

The intention is to add, for each CITY, its principal source of power. As an initial guess, use the principal source of power for the STATE. As more information is obtained, the data set will be updated for specific CITY observations. For one portion of the data, then, this is the intended scenario:

STATE	CITY	POWER
PA	HARRISBURG	OIL
PA	PHILADELPHIA	OIL
PA	PITTSBURGH	OIL
PA	THREE MILE ISLAND	NUCLEAR
PA	WILKES-BARRE	OIL
PA	WILLIAMSPORT	OIL

The programmer knows that POWER should be NUCLEAR for THREE MILE ISLAND, but adding this information in the same DATA step with the MERGE can produce the wrong result:

```
DATA COMBINED;
MERGE CITIES (IN=KEEPME) POWER;
BY STATE;
IF KEEPME;
IF STATE = 'PA' AND CITY = 'THREE MILE ISLAND'
THEN POWER = 'NUCLEAR';
```

Since the value of POWER is retained, rather than reread, this is the result:

STATE	CITY	POWER
PA	HARRISBURG	OIL
PA	PHILADELPHIA	OIL
PA	PITTSBURGH	OIL
PA	THREE MILE ISLAND	NUCLEAR
PA	WILKES-BARRE	NUCLEAR
PA	WILLIAMSPORT	NUCLEAR

There would be no warning or error message. Instead, the final data set would be incorrect. Once you recognize the problem, the solution is fairly straightforward: create a new variable based on POWER:

```
DATA COMBINED;
MERGE CITIES (IN=KEEPME) POWER;
BY STATE;
IF KEEPME;
IF NOT (STATE = 'PA' AND CITY = 'THREE MILE ISLAND')
THEN NEWVAR = POWER;
ELSE NEWVAR = 'NUCLEAR';
DROP POWER;
RENAME NEWVAR = POWER;
```

Note: The statements should be used in order, assigning

```
NEWVAR = POWER
```

before

```
NEWVAR = 'NUCLEAR'
```

In that way, NEWVAR receives the same length as POWER. If the order were reversed, NEWVAR would be defined as seven characters long (the number of characters in "NUCLEAR").

PART 2

50 TOUGHER PROBLEMS

Here are the stumpers, the brain teasers, the problems that separate the upper echelon SAS programmers from the want-to-bes. At last, we're on to the good stuff! These are the problems that often have stumped senior-level programmers across the country. In fact, if you want to further challenge yourself, see if you can beat the ideal times shown in the stopwatches.

Some problems are easier than others. There is no particular pattern to the order of the problems. As in Part 1, each problem lists related tools and concepts, which are cross-referenced in the appendix. Once again, cover up the list if you don't want any hints.

A Splendid Array

This program worked when tested, yet when run the next day against production data, it ended with a SAS error message. Both the test and production data sets contain the same variables, with identical attributes. How could this happen?

```
DATA _NULL_;
SET CITIES END=EOF;
BY STATE;
RETAIN COUNT1-COUNT50 0;
ARRAY COUNTS {50} COUNT1-COUNT50;
DUMMY + FIRST.STATE;
IF INDEX(CITY,'VILLE') THEN COUNTS{DUMMY} + 1;
IF EOF THEN DO DUMMY = 1 TO 50;
    PUT 'TOTAL NUMBER OF CITIES IN STATE '
        DUMMY
        'CONTAINING "VILLE" IS ' COUNTS{DUMMY};
END;
```

Tools and concepts:

Arrays

Customized reporting

RETAIN statement/Sum statement

```
DATA _NULL_;
SET CITIES END=EOF;
BY STATE;
RETAIN COUNT1-COUNT50 0;
ARRAY COUNTS {50} COUNT1-COUNT50;
DUMMY + FIRST.STATE;
IF INDEX(CITY,'VILLE') THEN COUNTS{DUMMY} + 1;
IF EOF THEN DO DUMMY = 1 TO 50;
   PUT 'TOTAL NUMBER OF CITIES IN STATE '
      DUMMY
         'CONTAINING "VILLE" IS ' COUNTS{DUMMY};
END;
```

The production data set contained more than 50 values for STATE. As a result, DUMMY took on a value of 51. At that point, since the program uses DUMMY as the index of a 50-element array, the reference to COUNTS{DUMMY} generated an error message.

On a side note, these two statements would produce equivalent results as long as FIRST.STATE is either 0 or 1:

```
DUMMY + FIRST.STATE;
IF FIRST.STATE THEN DUMMY + 1;
```

The first is a little more difficult to interpret, but it could not have produced an error.

PROBLEM 22

I'll Give You My Number

Data entry clerks used many different styles for entering telephone numbers. Some typical styles:

```
(999) 999-9999
999-999-9999
999/999-9999
999 999 9999
```

This statement attempted to standardize the data, obtaining 10 digits:

```
PHONE = COMPRESS(PHONE, '() -/');
```

However, the next time around one data entry clerk used a backslash (\) instead of a slash (/), and one used square brackets ([ ]) instead of parentheses (( )). Instead of updating the program each time a new batch of data arrives, modify the program to guarantee that it selects only numeric digits, removing all other characters. (Extra credit for simplicity and elegance.)

Tools and concepts:

Functions

```
PHONE = COMPRESS(PHONE, '() -/');
```

COMPRESS works in the original program by removing any instances of characters mentioned in the second parameter.

One way to remove extraneous characters is to replace all non-digits with blanks, and then remove the blanks:

```
IF PHONE > ' ' THEN DO I = 1 TO LENGTH(PHONE);
   IF SUBSTR(PHONE, I, 1) NOT IN
   ('0','1','2','3','4','5','6','7','8','9')
   THEN SUBSTR(PHONE, I, 1) = ' ';
END;
PHONE = COMPRESS(PHONE);
```

When the second parameter is not specified, COMPRESS removes all blanks. Many variations exist on this technique. For example:

1. Both the ASCII and EBCDIC collating sequences run directly from 0 through 9, with no non-digits in between. Therefore, the IN operator could be replaced by:

   ```
   NOT ('0' <= SUBSTR(PHONE, I, 1) <= '9')
   ```

2. Instead of replacing non-digits with blanks, it would be possible to create 10 character variables each one character long. Take the first 10 digits found and assign them as the values of these new variables. Finally, concatenate the new variables to generate the final value for PHONE. One possible danger with this approach: perhaps the original PHONE variable contains more than 10 digits (either bad data or an international number).

For extra credit (worth half of a correct solution), consider this statement:

```
NEWVAR = COMPRESS(PHONE, '0123456789');
```

It retrieves all non-digits from the original PHONE variable. That's half of an elegant solution! If you can obtain the non-digits, you can remove them with:

```
PHONE = COMPRESS(PHONE,
            COMPRESS(PHONE, '0123456789'));
```

Lowest Score Wins

In the following merge, both data sets contain the variable STROKES. Rewrite the program to achieve the following objectives:

1. Don't change the number of observations in GOLF.

2. On each observation, the value of STROKES should be the lower of the two incoming values, excluding missing values.

3. Allow for many-to-one merges.

```
DATA GOLF;
MERGE FRONT9 BACK9;
BY SSN;
```

Data set options
MERGE statement

```
DATA GOLF;
MERGE FRONT9 BACK9;
BY SSN;
```

If this were a one-to-one merge, the solution would be simple. Rename one of the STROKES variables so that comparisons could be made. For example, assuming no special numeric missing values such as .A:

```
DATA GOLF;
MERGE FRONT9 BACK9 (RENAME=(STROKES=B_STROKE));
BY SSN;
IF STROKES = . OR (. < B_STROKE < STROKES)
THEN STROKES = B_STROKE;
```

However, this approach can fail in a many-to-one merge. Consider these incoming data sets:

FRONT9			BACK9			GOLF	
SSN	STROKES		SSN	STROKES		SSN	STROKES
1	85		1	90		1	85
			1	70		1	70
			1	75		1	70 (not 75)

Here, because STROKES gets retained in memory, rather than reread from FRONT9, STROKES remains 70 as the program begins the third observation. That observation selects the lower of 70 or 75. If you knew that BACK9 would always be the "many" data set in the many-to-one merge, you could rename the STROKES variable from FRONT9 instead. However, if you don't know which is the "many" data set, it becomes necessary to rename BOTH variables:

```
DATA GOLF;
MERGE FRONT9 (RENAME=(STROKES=F_STROKE))
      BACK9  (RENAME=(STROKES=B_STROKE));
BY SSN;
IF      B_STROKE = . THEN STROKES = F_STROKE;
ELSE IF F_STROKE = . THEN STROKES = B_STROKE;
ELSE IF (B_STROKE < F_STROKE)
THEN STROKES = B_STROKE;
ELSE STROKES = F_STROKE;
```

First Doesn't Succeed

This program creates a macro variable counting the total number of states. As is, the program works. However, if the program replaced LAST.STATE with FIRST.STATE, the program would fail most of the time but occasionally would work. Why would this happen?

```
DATA _NULL_;
SET COUNTRY (KEEP=STATE) END=EOF;
BY STATE;
IF LAST.STATE;
N + 1;
IF EOF THEN CALL SYMPUT
('NSTATES', TRIM(LEFT(PUT(N, 2.))));
```

Macro language

Subsetting IF/DELETE

```
DATA _NULL_;
SET COUNTRY (KEEP=STATE) END=EOF;
BY STATE;
IF LAST.STATE;
N + 1;
IF EOF THEN CALL SYMPUT
('NSTATES', TRIM(LEFT(PUT(N, 2.))));
```

The problem is one of detecting end-of-file when deleting observations with a subsetting IF. The subsetting IF never deletes the last observation in the original program. After all, the last observation in the data set must be the last one for one of the states. When substituting FIRST.STATE for LAST.STATE, however, the program very likely will delete the last observation. The only time this won't happen is when the last STATE has only one observation in COUNTRY. If the last observation does get deleted, the final statement never executes for that observation. There would not be an error message; the DATA step merely would end without having created the macro variable NSTATES.

The appendix lists this problem under "Detecting end-of-file," although the list of tools and concepts on the previous page does not. That would have been too big a hint.

An interesting side issue is the use of the TRIM function. Prior to Release 6.08, the LEFT function would not only left-hand justify a character string, but it would remove trailing blanks as well. In effect, it removed both leading and trailing blanks, making the TRIM function unnecessary. Beginning with Release 6.08, however, LEFT merely left-hand justifies a character string. If trailing blanks would cause a problem, the program must use the TRIM function to remove them. When the second argument contains no embedded blanks, COMPRESS can replace the combination of TRIM and LEFT.

PROBLEM 25

What's That Number Again?

Where and why does the error occur in this program?

```
PROC FORMAT;
PICTURE NUMPHONE
   OTHER = ' 999) 999-9999' (PREFIX='(');

DATA TESTFORM;
PHONE = '6179380307';
NUMPHONE = INPUT(PHONE,$10.);

PROC PRINT DATA=TESTFORM;
FORMAT NUMPHONE NUMPHONE.;
```

```
PROC FORMAT;
PICTURE NUMPHONE
   OTHER = ' 999) 999-9999' (PREFIX='(');

DATA TESTFORM;
PHONE = '6179380307';
NUMPHONE = INPUT(PHONE,$10.);

PROC PRINT DATA=TESTFORM;
FORMAT NUMPHONE NUMPHONE.;
```

The error occurs on the last statement because the variable NUMPHONE is a character variable while the format NUMPHONE is numeric.

The mistake occurs when creating the variable NUMPHONE by using the wrong informat. The INPUT function should take a character string as the first parameter. The second parameter (the informat) can be either character or numeric. Using the $10. informat creates NUMPHONE as character. Using the 10. informat would have (properly) created NUMPHONE as numeric. In a very similar fashion, both INPUT statements below are capable of reading 10 digits. The first creates VARNAME as character while the second creates VARNAME as numeric:

```
INPUT VARNAME $10.;
INPUT VARNAME 10.;
```

The INPUT function works the same way, determining the attributes of the new variable from the informat that reads its value.

PROBLEM 26

Reread That Section

Sketch the final data set.

```
DATA SECTION;
DO A = 1 TO 10;
   OUTPUT;
   B = A;
END;

DATA FINAL;
SET SECTION;
IF A > 5;
SET SECTION (KEEP=B);
```

Tools and concepts:

DATA step flow
Subsetting IF/DELETE

When a DATA step contains multiple SET statements, each acts independently of the other(s). In the second DATA step, each SET statement

- begins by reading the first observation from SECTION, and

- continues by reading the next observation, disregarding the actions of the other SET statement.

The subsetting IF deletes observations containing small values for the variable A. The second SET executes only when A > 5. Here is the process:

	Value of A	Value of B	Delete Observation?
1st SET	1	.	Yes
1st SET	2	1	Yes
1st SET	3	2	Yes
1st SET	4	3	Yes
1st SET	5	4	Yes
1st SET	6	5	
2nd SET	6	.	No
1st SET	7	6	
2nd SET	7	1	No
1st SET	8	7	
2nd SET	8	2	No
1st SET	9	8	
2nd SET	9	3	No
1st SET	10	9	
2nd SET	10	4	No

The five observations marked "No" make up the FINAL data set.

PROBLEM 27

The Final Word

Raw data contain an unusual form of packed numbers. Somehow, the last word of the last byte contains a random set of bits, rather than the standard hex C or D. How can you read in a three-byte packed number where the last word is an unknown, perhaps random, series of bits? These sample data values from columns 1 to 3 of the raw data should provide the value 21,548:

        2 5 8
        1 4 ?

Notes:

- All data values should be positive integers.

- The term "word" refers to the first or last four bits within each byte.

Tools and concepts:

Functions
Reading raw data

Columns 1 to 3 of the raw data should provide the value 21,548:

2 5 8
1 4 ?

The raw data can be read as two variables, using different informats. Consider this as a beginning:

```
INPUT  @1 PART1  PK2.   @3 PART2 IB1.;
```

Now each variable contains a portion of the final number. PART1 needs to be multiplied by 10, while PART2 needs the final 4 bits to be dropped. Let's take a more in-depth look at the value of PART2:

Bit within Column 3	Value Added to PART2
8	0 or 1
7	0 or 2
6	0 or 4
5	0 or 8
4	0 or 16
3	0 or 32
2	0 or 64
1	0 or 128

Adjusting the value of PART2 requires two steps. The final four bits (5 through 8) must be dropped, while the first four bits (1 through 4) must be adjusted as follows. The fourth bit, instead of adding 0 (if off) or 16 (if on), should add 0 or 1. The third bit, instead of adding 0 or 32, should add 0 or 2. The second bit should add 0 or 4, and the first bit should add 0 or 8. So the program full program would be the following:

```
INPUT  @1 PART1  PK2.  @3 PART2 IB1.;
PART1 = PART1 * 10;
PART2 = INT(PART2/16);
```

All that is left to do is to put the pieces back together:

```
VALUE = PART1 + PART2;
```

Notes:

- The PK family of informats reads each word, converting it to a positive integer.

- The PK3. informat could not read the entire string if the last word contained a value greater than 9.

- If the actual value of the last word is significant, calculate it before resetting the value of PART2:

```
LASTWORD = MOD(PART2, 16);
```

Another equally valid approach is possible. Consider the following:

```
INPUT  @1 STRING $CHAR3.;
VALUE = INPUT(PUT(STRING,$HEX6.),5.);
```

The INPUT statement can read any characters. Now the PUT function expresses each word as a separate HEX digit, including the last word, which may or may not be a base 10 digit. Regardless, the INPUT function can easily read the first five digits, ignoring the sixth.

Having alternative methods is particularly valuable if you try to verify your answers using a computer. You don't need a mainframe and you don't need packed data. Instead, you can type in a few random characters as the data lines and see if the two methods produce the same answer. Even if the characters you type contain invalid data, both methods should pick up on that situation.

Believe it or not, this type of problem has occurred in real life in two entirely different scenarios:

1. In one case, raw data were generated by a third generation language that should have put out the data in packed form. Instead, the last word contained a nonstandard set of values.

2. In another case, disk space was incredibly tight. To save on space, positive numbers were written out in packed form, without using a word to indicate the sign. However, five-digit numbers did not require the sixth word. Therefore, the sixth word was used to hold the first digit of the next piece of information. A byte could contain the last digit of one variable plus the first digit of the next variable.

PROBLEM 28

A Staggered Start

The second program attempts to emulate the FIRSTOBS= option in the first program. Assuming OLD contains 100 observations, describe NEW for both programs.

```
OPTIONS FIRSTOBS=5;        DATA NEW;
                           DO UNTIL ( _N_ >= 5);
                              SET OLD;
DATA NEW;                  END;
SET OLD;
```

Tools and concepts:

　　　DATA step flow
　　　DO loops

```
     OPTIONS FIRSTOBS=5;          DATA NEW;
                                  DO UNTIL ( _N_ >= 5);
     DATA NEW;                       SET OLD;
     SET OLD;                     END;
```

The first DATA step generates 96 observations, the fifth through 100th from OLD. FIRSTOBS= causes the DATA step to begin reading with the fifth observation from any source of data (in this case, the data set OLD).

The second DATA step generates zero observations. _N_ measures the number of times the program leaves the DATA statement. _N_ does not measure the number of observations read from OLD. The DATA step on the right enters the DO loop and reads every observation from OLD, all with _N_=1; therefore, nothing has been output by the time the SET statement runs out of observations to read and the DATA step ends.

PROBLEM 29

How Long Is a Piece of String?

What are the values of L1, L2, L3, and L4?

```
DATA NEW;
STRING  = REPEAT('X ', 50);
L1 = LENGTH(STRING);
L2 = LENGTH(REPEAT(STRING, 1));
L3 = LENGTH(COMPRESS(REPEAT('X ', 150)));
L4 = LENGTH(STRING || STRING);
```

Tools and concepts:

Functions

Lengths of variables

```
DATA NEW;
STRING  = REPEAT('X ',  50);
L1 = LENGTH(STRING);
L2 = LENGTH(REPEAT(STRING, 1));
L3 = LENGTH(COMPRESS(REPEAT('X ', 150)));
L4 = LENGTH(STRING || STRING);
```

The first set of issues concerns the REPEAT function. Some key features are

- ■ The REPEAT function takes an original character string and repeats it a specified number of ADDITIONAL times.

- ■ When the REPEAT function defines a new variable, that variable is automatically assigned a length of 200, the maximum possible for a character variable.

Therefore, the value of STRING is a series of 51 occurrences of X and is padded with blanks to reach a length of 200. The last X appears in position 101. L1 has a value of 101.

L2 also has a value of 101. In theory, the REPEAT function produces a character string that is 400 characters long. In practice, the software only works with a maximum of 200 characters. Since STRING contains 200 characters, the repeated characters are lost.

L3 is 100. The first 200 characters generated by the REPEAT function are fed to the COMPRESS function. Once blanks have been removed, 100 characters remain.

L4 is (surprisingly) 255. Evidently, the concatenated characters are stored in a buffer larger than 200 characters. Do not count L4 when grading your score for this problem. The only way to know its value is to run the program and examine the results. The original problem-solving contest also disregarded L4, using it only to determine if a contest participant used a computer.

A Random Selection?

This program selects a 25-observation random sample (with replacement). Yet, when run many times against differently sized data sets, an unusual pattern emerged. The smaller data sets had a greater chance of having the same observation selected twice. That's to be expected; however, the same observation was being selected twice in a row twice as often as the laws of probability would dictate. Why would this happen?

```
DATA SELECT25;
DO I = 1 TO 25;
    GETME = INT(TOTOBS * RANUNI(0));
    SET HUGE.FILE POINT=GETME NOBS=TOTOBS;
    OUTPUT;
END;
STOP;
```

Functions

SET statement options

```
DATA SELECT25;
DO I = 1 TO 25;
   GETME = INT(TOTOBS * RANUNI(0));
   SET HUGE.FILE POINT=GETME NOBS=TOTOBS;
   OUTPUT;
END;
STOP;
```

The program illustrates many correct tools, and nearly accomplishes its objectives. The DO loop selects and outputs 25 observations, and then halts the DATA step. Without the STOP statement, the DATA step would have continued with a second (and a third, and many more) iteration of the DO loop.

The DO loop identifies which observation to select. The formula for GETME nearly does the job correctly:

1. RANUNI generates a random number uniformly distributed between 0 and 1.

2. TOTOBS already exists before the SET statement executes because the NOBS= option on the SET statement assigns TOTOBS its value as the DATA step statements get compiled, not as they execute.

3. Multiplying the two together generates a random number uniformly distributed between 0 and the total number of observations in the data set.

4. The INT function converts this number to an integer so that POINT= on the SET statement can retrieve that particular observation. Here is where the mistake creeps in: since the INT function truncates, it can return a value of 0.

The mistake is using the INT function rather than the CEIL function, which would have rounded up to the next highest integer. (If the CEIL function receives an integer value as the argument, it returns that same integer, not the next highest integer.) When GETME has a value of 0, the SET statement does not retrieve an observation. Instead, the values read by the previous iteration of the DO loop get output a second time.

PROBLEM 31

The End Is Near

Write a quick, inexpensive program to print the last observation of the data set ALL. You can assume that ALL contains approximately 100,000 observations and is stored on disk.

Tools and concepts:

OUTPUT statement

SET statement options

The previous problem, "A Random Selection?", illustrated how the SET statement can use the NOBS= option to discover how many observations are in a data set and the POINT= option to retrieve a specific observation. This program uses similar tools:

```
DATA JUSTLAST;
SET HUGEFILE NOBS=TOTOBS POINT=TOTOBS;
OUTPUT;
STOP;


PROC PRINT DATA=JUSTLAST;
```

As before

- NOBS= creates TOTOBS at compile time, before the SET statement executes.

- the STOP statement halts the DATA step, preventing it from continuing to output the same observation time after time.

The program needs an OUTPUT statement; otherwise, STOP would halt the DATA step before it output any observations.

If HUGEFILE were sorted by AMOUNT, similar programming techniques could compute percentiles. For example, to compute the median amount:

```
DATA MEDIAN;
SET HUGEFILE NOBS=TOTOBS;
OBSNO = (TOTOBS + 1) / 2;
IF OBSNO = INT(OBSNO) THEN DO;
   SET HUGEFILE POINTS=OBSNO;
   MEDIAN = AMOUNT;
   OUTPUT;
   STOP;
END;
DO I = OBSNO - 0.5 TO OBSNO + 0.5;
   SET HUGEFILE POINT=I;
   TOTAL + AMOUNT;
END;
MEDIAN = TOTAL / 2;
OUTPUT;
STOP;
```

PROBLEM 32

If You Can Read This...

Sketch the final data set COMBINED.

```
DATA CITIES1;
INPUT CITY $ STATE $;
CARDS;
MIAMI FLORIDA
HOUSTON TEXAS
AUSTIN TEXAS
;

DATA CITIES2;
INPUT CITY $9.;
CARDS;
NEWARK
NASHVILLE
;

DATA COMBINED;
SET CITIES1 CITIES2;
IF CITY = 'NEWARK' THEN STATE = 'NEW JERSEY';
```

Tools and concepts:
Lengths of variables
RETAIN statement/Sum statement

The three DATA steps establish the length of CITY in three different ways:

1. Since the first DATA step creates CITY and STATE by scanning across the line of raw data, both variables automatically receive a length of 8.

2. Since the second DATA step uses the $9. informat, CITY receives a length of 9.

3. Since the third DATA step mentions CITIES1 first, CITY receives a length of 8.

The final data set, then, truncates CITY and STATE down to a length of 8:

```
CITY        STATE


MIAMI       FLORIDA
HOUSTON     TEXAS
AUSTIN      TEXAS
NEWARK      NEW JERS
NASHVILL    NEW JERS
```

Notice that STATE remains NEW JERS for the final observation. This result represents a change introduced in Version 6 of the SAS System, resulting from this combination of factors:

1. CITIES2 does not contain STATE.

2. Since CITIES1 contains STATE, STATE gets retained.

When the SET statement concatenates data sets, when should the software reinitialize variables read from other data sets? The answer used to be "for every observation." Now the answer is "when reading the first observation from each data set."

Bigger Is Better

This program attempts to extract all cities in states that contain a large city (population of 1 million or more). Why won't the program work? Be very specific about how you would fix it.

```
DATA BIGSTATE;
MERGE ALL
      ALL (WHERE=(POP >= 1000000) IN=BIG);
BY STATE;
IF BIG;
```

Data set options
MERGE statement

A program can merge a data set with itself, as long as the data reside on disk. Each mention of the data set is treated as if a different data set were being referenced. Consider the following similar program instead:

```
DATA BIGSTATE;
MERGE ALL LARGE (IN=BIG);
BY STATE;
IF BIG;
```

This program is a standard programming technique to select the proper observations from the sources below:

```
<<<<<< ALL >>>>>>        LARGE

STATE         POP        STATE

AL          50000        NY
AL          90000
NY          75000
NY        1000000
NY         150000
```

The original program faces a very similar scenario. However, the equivalent of the LARGE data set contains a second variable, POP. There is no way to get rid of POP because it is referenced in the WHERE clause.

```
<<<<<< ALL >>>>>>        <<<<< LARGE >>>>>

STATE         POP        STATE         POP

AL          50000        NY          1000000
AL          90000
NY          75000
NY        1000000
NY         150000
```

MERGE now overwrites the value of 75,000 with a value of 1,000,000 for the first NY observation. One of the easier solutions is to switch the order of the data sets in the MERGE statement so that 75,000 overwrites 1,000,000:

```
DATA BIGSTATE;
MERGE ALL (WHERE=(POP >= 1000000) IN=BIG)
      ALL;
BY STATE;
IF BIG;
```

PROBLEM 34

It's Elementary

The DATA step ran without error. However, PROC PRINT generated an error message. What is the mystery statement?

```
DATA NEW;
SET CITIES;
BY STATE;
*MYSTERY STATEMENT;
DENSTIY = POP / AREA;

PROC PRINT DATA=NEW;
BY STATE;
```

```
DATA NEW;
SET CITIES;
BY STATE;
*MYSTERY STATEMENT;
DENSTIY = POP / AREA;

PROC PRINT DATA=NEW;
BY STATE;
```

Many mystery statements are possible. Most would cause the data to enter the DATA step in order but leave out of order. Any of these statements could cause a later error:

```
IF LAST.STATE THEN STATE = ' ';
IF RANUNI(0) < 0.2 THEN STATE = ' ';
IF STATE = 'AL' THEN STATE = 'ZZ';
RENAME STATE=NEWNAME;
```

The primary message here is that NEW may not be in sorted order. The BY statement in the DATA step examines the observations as they enter, not as they leave. Even in a simple DATA step (such as the one above but without a mystery statement), the SAS System has no guarantee that the output data set is in sorted order.

This result implies that you should code the SORTEDBY= data set option. Current releases of the software store the sorted order of a data set as header information. In the program below, the SAS System double-checks that sorted order, and automatically skips the PROC SORT:

```
DATA NEW (SORTEDBY=STATE);
SET CITIES;
BY STATE;
DENSITY = POP / AREA;

PROC SORT DATA=NEW;
BY STATE;
```

Without the SORTEDBY= option, the SAS System would have executed the PROC SORT.

Animal Magic

When this program ran, the final value of TOTAL was 4, not 2. How could this have happened?

```
DATA ANIMALS;
INPUT BUFFALO YAK OX;
IF BUFFALO = 0 THEN TOTAL + 1;
IF YAK     = 0 THEN TOTAL + 1;
IF OX      = 0 THEN TOTAL + 1;
CARDS;
0 255 16
8 0 1024
;
```

Tools and concepts:

None

```
DATA ANIMALS;
INPUT BUFFALO YAK OX;
IF BUFFALO = 0 THEN TOTAL + 1;
IF YAK     = 0 THEN TOTAL + 1;
IF 0X      = 0 THEN TOTAL + 1;
CARDS;
0 255 16
8 0 1024
;
```

TOTAL is 4 because the program contains a typographical error. These two are different:

OX = the variable name

0X = the hex literal value 0

The third IF / THEN statement increments TOTAL regardless of the value of the variable OX.

Haven't I Seen You Somewhere Before?

How could this program have produced the output below?

```
PROC SUMMARY DATA=SALES;
BY STATE;
VAR AMOUNT;
OUTPUT OUT=STATS SUM=TOTSALES;

PROC PRINT DATA=STATS NOOBS;
VAR STATE TOTSALES;
```

STATE	TOTSALES
MAINE	2500
MASSACHUSETTS	1300
NEW HAMPSHIRE	3800
MAINE	2200
NEW HAMPSHIRE	6000

Formats
PROC MEANS/PROC SUMMARY

```
STATE                TOTSALES


MAINE                2500
MASSACHUSETTS        1300
NEW HAMPSHIRE        3800
MAINE                2200
NEW HAMPSHIRE        6000
```

The data set STATS seems to contain three values for STATE but actually contains five unique values. These are formatted values for STATE rather than actual stored values. The preliminary setup may have been the following:

```
PROC FORMAT;
VALUE STNAME 1, 4 = 'MAINE'
                2 = 'MASSACHUSETTS'
             3, 5 = 'NEW HAMPSHIRE';


DATA SALES;
SET SALES;
FORMAT STATE STNAME.;
```

Notes:

- If consecutive values of STATE both belonged to the same formatted value of STATE, those values would have been combined into a single observation in the output data set.

- If a CLASS statement were used instead of a BY statement, there would have been just one observation per formatted value of STATE in the output data set.

- The MVS environment supports the CAPSOUT option, which uppercases all printed output. That option provides a correct (albeit obscure) solution, given that the original data contained some uppercase and some lowercase values.

You Can Call Me Paul

The second program attempts to emulate the WHERE statement in the first program. Why didn't it work? How would you fix it? (You can assume that N does not exist in ALLNAMES.)

```
DATA SUBSET1;              DATA SUBSET2;
SET ALLNAMES;             DO UNTIL (NAME='PAUL');
WHERE NAME = 'PAUL';          SET ALLNAMES (KEEP=NAME);
                              N + 1;
                          END;
                          SET ALLNAMES POINT=N;
```

DATA step flow
Lengths of variables
Macro language
WHERE statement

```
DATA SUBSET2;
DO UNTIL (NAME='PAUL');
   SET ALLNAMES (KEEP=NAME);
   N + 1;
END;
SET ALLNAMES POINT=N;
```

This program represents a valiant effort because of the operation of the SET statements. Each SET statement operates independently of the other. The first SET statement tracks which observations have already been read by that SET statement; each time it executes, it reads in the next observation from ALLNAMES. This feature remains true whether many observations are read in the DO loop, or whether the DATA step programming statements end, the program returns to the DATA statement, and the DATA step continues executing. These are the major actions taken by the program:

1. Leave the DATA statement, enter the DO loop, and read NAME from one observation in ALLNAMES. Use the variable N to count which observation was read. (DO UNTIL never checks whether the condition is true or false until reaching the END statement. Thus even if NAME is already PAUL before the loop begins, the SET statement still executes.)

2. Continue this process until an observation contains NAME=PAUL.

3. Leave the loop, and read in all variables from that observation.

4. Upon reaching the end of the programming statements, return to the DATA statement and output the current observation.

This process repeats until the first SET statement fails because it runs out of observations to read from ALLNAMES. When the SET statement fails, the DATA step ends. That is a normal ending to a DATA step.

How could these results differ from using a WHERE statement? The problem lies in the length of the variable NAME. The program above first mentions NAME by comparing it to PAUL. Since PAUL is only four characters long, this defines NAME as being four characters long. Therefore, the SET statement truncates the values it reads. The program selects any observation where NAME began with PAUL before truncation, such as PAULA, PAULINE, and PAULETTE.

A number of solutions are possible. Assuming you want to eliminate as a possibility the original WHERE statement (as well as a subsetting IF), you need some way to define the length of NAME properly. One method is to add a third SET statement:

```
DATA SUBSET3;
IF 0 THEN SET ALLNAMES;
DO UNTIL (NAME='PAUL');
   SET ALLNAMES (KEEP=NAME);
   N + 1;
END;
SET ALLNAMES POINT=N;
```

The condition 0 is universally false, so the first SET statement never executes. However, the statement still has an effect when the DATA step gets compiled. Every variable in ALLNAMES gets defined, including assigning NAME a length. When the DO UNTIL statement gets compiled, NAME already exists and keeps its length attribute.

Examining the program above suggests an interesting rearrangement of the statements. Since a condition (0) gets checked every time you find the NAME PAUL, why not make the check a useful one? Here is the code that will perform that check:

```
DATA SUBSET4;
IF N THEN DO;
   SET ALLNAMES POINT=N;
   OUTPUT;
END;
DO UNTIL (NAME='PAUL');
   SET ALLNAMES (KEEP=NAME);
   N + 1;
END;
```

N is initially 0 (a false condition) because of this statement:

```
N + 1;
```

Once the DO loop begins, N becomes a positive integer (a true condition). When the loop ends, the program returns to the DATA statement, outputs nothing (because the DATA step contains an OUTPUT statement), and continues executing. Next, the program finds that the condition N is true, and thus it retrieves and outputs the proper observation. As before, the DATA step ends when the second SET statement fails because ALLNAMES runs out of observations. One final approach assigns a longer length to NAME. This initial attempt would waste space, but would output the proper observations:

```
DATA SUBSET5;
LENGTH NAME $ 200;
DO UNTIL (NAME='PAUL');
   SET ALLNAMES (KEEP=NAME);
   N + 1;
END;
SET ALLNAMES POINT=N;
```

Using a few extra steps, a program could retrieve the actual length of NAME and supply that number to a LENGTH statement. PROC CONTENTS produces a data set with one observation for each variable in the original data set ALLNAMES:

```
PROC CONTENTS DATA=ALLNAMES NOPRINT
      OUT=TEMP (KEEP=NAME LENGTH);

DATA _NULL_;
SET TEMP;
WHERE NAME = 'NAME';
CALL SYMPUT('L', PUT(LENGTH,3.));

DATA SUBSET6;
LENGTH NAME $ &L;
DO UNTIL (NAME='PAUL');
   SET ALLNAMES (KEEP=NAME);
   N + 1;
END;
SET ALLNAMES POINT=N;
```

The data set TEMP contains NAME with values totally different from those in ALLNAMES. In TEMP, NAME takes on values such as AGE, HEIGHT, NAME, and WEIGHT. These values are the names of variables in ALLNAMES.

However, the solution is becoming longer and more complex. The earlier, simpler solutions are more appropriate for solving this problem. Nevertheless, advanced level programs often use PROC CONTENTS to create a data set holding information about existing variables, followed by a DATA step to capture that information as macro variables.

An Expression of Love

Which of these statements are guaranteed to generate an error message? For any that might work, explain the conditions that would be necessary to make them work.

```
FORMAT LOVE GIANTNAME.;
FORMAT LOVE F9_F10_F11.;
FORMAT LOVE F999F999.;
```

Tools and concepts:

Formats

```
FORMAT LOVE GIANTNAME.;
FORMAT LOVE F9_F10_F11.;
FORMAT LOVE F999F999.;
```

The third statement always generates an error. The first and second statements could work, despite the limitation of eight characters per format name.

When you mention a format name longer than eight letters, the extra letters get ignored. If the format GIANTNAM existed, the first format statement would work, and the program would use that format.

The VALUE statement in PROC FORMAT cannot use a format name ending in a number. The name F9, for example, is illegal. Actually, there's a logical reason for this limitation: it gives the programmer the flexibility to add a number later, when using the format, to control how many characters should print. Consider this format:

```
VALUE RATES   0 -    8 = 'LOWEST RATE'
              9 -   12 = 'MIDDLE RATE'
             13 - HIGH = 'HIGHEST RATE';
```

When printing, the program can refer to the RATES7. format, which will print the first seven characters of the RATES format.

In this problem, if the format F9_F10_F existed (and had a length of at least 11), the second FORMAT statement would be requesting that the first 11 characters of the formatted value be printed.

The last statement never works. Even if the format F999F existed, the width of 999 would be wider still than the maximum width of 200 characters.

PROBLEM 39

Twins?

Under what circumstances do these programs produce identical results?

```
DATA ANSWERS;
SET SURVEY END=EOF;
IF       ANSWER = 1 THEN A + 1;
ELSE IF ANSWER = 2 THEN B + 1;
ELSE IF ANSWER = 3 THEN C + 1;
IF EOF;
KEEP A B C;


DATA ANSWERS;
SET SURVEY END=EOF;
ARRAY COUNTER {3} A B C;
COUNTER{ANSWER} + 1;
IF EOF;
KEEP A B C;
```

Tools and concepts:

  Arrays
  RETAIN statement/Sum statement

```
DATA ANSWERS;
SET SURVEY END=EOF;
IF       ANSWER = 1 THEN A + 1;
ELSE IF ANSWER = 2 THEN B + 1;
ELSE IF ANSWER = 3 THEN C + 1;
IF EOF;
KEEP A B C;


DATA ANSWERS;
SET SURVEY END=EOF;
ARRAY COUNTER {3} A B C;
COUNTER{ANSWER} + 1;
IF EOF;
KEEP A B C;
```

Much of the time, the programs produce identical results. The variable A counts the number of times ANSWER=1, while B and C count values of 2 and 3. Both programs retain these counters as the DATA step moves through the incoming data. When could differences occur? Only when the data fail to behave in the following ways:

- If ANSWER never takes on a particular value. For example, if ANSWER never takes on a value of 1, the final value of A is 0 with the first program, but missing with the second.

- If ANSWER takes on illegal subscript values. For example, if ANSWER is 5 on a given observation, the first program ignores the observation while the second program returns an execution time error.

- If ANSWER takes on noninteger values. For example, if ANSWER is 2.8 on a given observation, the first program ignores the observation while the second program increments B.

As a general rule, better programmers allow for the unexpected.

Take full credit for a correct solution if you got two out of the three conditions.

A Name Game

Which statements below print the word MATCH?

```
DATA _NULL_;
NAME1 = 'AL';
NAME2 = 'ALAN';
NAME3 = 'ALBERT';
PREFIX = SUBSTR(NAME3,1,2);
IF NAME1 =: PREFIX THEN PUT 'MATCH';
IF NAME2 =: PREFIX THEN PUT 'MATCH';
IF NAME3 =: PREFIX THEN PUT 'MATCH';
```

Tools and concepts:

Functions

Lengths of variables

```
DATA _NULL_;
NAME1 = 'AL';
NAME2 = 'ALAN';
NAME3 = 'ALBERT';
PREFIX = SUBSTR(NAME3,1,2);
IF NAME1 =: PREFIX THEN PUT 'MATCH';
IF NAME2 =: PREFIX THEN PUT 'MATCH';
IF NAME3 =: PREFIX THEN PUT 'MATCH';
```

Only the first comparison produces a match.

Here are the two key issues:

1. What is the length of PREFIX?
   Whenever the SUBSTR function creates a variable, it gives that variable the length of the incoming character string. Thus PREFIX has a length of 6, consisting of the letters AL followed by four blanks.

2. What does the comparison operator =: mean?
   It compares two character strings to see if they are equal. However, if one string has a shorter length than the other, the SAS System truncates the longer string down to the length of the shorter string.

To make the first comparison, the software truncates PREFIX (the longer string) down to a length of 2 (the length of NAME1). The two strings are then equal.

To make the second comparison, the software truncates PREFIX (the longer string) down to a length of 4 (the length of NAME2). The two strings are not equal since the third and fourth characters are different.

To make the third comparison, no truncation is necessary. Both strings are 6 characters long, and they are not equal.

Drinkers See Double

Replace each pair of statements with a single statement. If the value you produce for DRINKER isn't exactly the same as what is produced now, explain the difference.

```
IF AGE > 21 THEN DRINKER = 1;
ELSE DRINKER = 2;

IF AGE > 21 THEN DRINKER = 'YES';
ELSE DRINKER = 'NO';
```

```
IF AGE > 21 THEN DRINKER = 1;
ELSE DRINKER = 2;

IF AGE > 21 THEN DRINKER = 'YES';
ELSE DRINKER = 'NO';
```

A variety of statements could replace the first two. Take advantage of the fact that the SAS System replaces true comparisons with 1 and false comparisons with 0. Any of these statements would do the trick:

```
DRINKER = 1 + (AGE <= 21);
DRINKER = (AGE > 21) + 2 * (AGE <= 21);
DRINKER = 2 - (AGE > 21);
```

The second group of statements builds upon these tools. For example:

```
DRINKER = SUBSTR('NO YES', 1 + 3 * (AGE > 21), 3);
```

The results are nearly identical to the original. Although SUBSTR retrieves three characters, the length of DRINKER is 6 (the length of the incoming character string).

Handle with Care

What does CAREFUL contain?

```
DATA TEMP;
DO A = 1 TO 5;
    OUTPUT;
END;

DATA CAREFUL;
B = LAG(A);
SET TEMP;
A = LAG(A);
```

```
DATA TEMP;
DO A = 1 TO 5;
   OUTPUT;
END;

DATA CAREFUL;
B = LAG(A);
SET TEMP;
A = LAG(A);
```

The LAG function does not mean "the value from the previous observation." Instead, it retrieves the value A had the last time that particular LAG function executed. The key to solving this problem is to list the value of A at the time each LAG function executes. Begin with the second LAG function, which gives you the value of A in the final data set:

Value of A at time of 2nd LAG	A = Value Returned by 2nd LAG Function
1	.
2	1
3	2
4	3
5	4

These results help establish the value of A when the first LAG function executes. Since A is read by a SET statement, its value is retained as each new observation begins:

Value of A at time of 1st LAG	B = Value Returned by 1st LAG Function
.	.
.	.
1	.
2	1
3	2

B is really LAG3(A). Each of these conditions creates a lag effect:

- using the first LAG function to compute B.
- resetting A by using the second LAG function.
- computing B before the SET statement.

The Big Apple

The following statements, when embedded within a macro, generated MATCH #1 but not MATCH #2. How could this have happened?

```
%IF &CITY = NEW YORK %THEN %PUT MATCH #1;

%IF "&CITY" = "NEW YORK" %THEN %PUT MATCH #2;
```

Macro language

```
%IF &CITY = NEW YORK %THEN %PUT MATCH #1;

%IF "&CITY" = "NEW YORK" %THEN %PUT MATCH #2;
```

Consider these statements first:

```
%IF NEW YORK        = NEW YORK %THEN %PUT MATCH #1;
```
Macro language would automatically ignore the trailing blanks and would find that the two character strings are equal.

```
%IF "NEW YORK  " = "NEW YORK" %THEN %PUT MATCH #2;
```
Macro language compares all characters, including the trailing blanks inside the quotes as well as the quotation marks themselves. The result: no match.

Now let's return to the original problem. The macro variable &CITY contains trailing blanks as part of its value. The first statement resolves &CITY, generates trailing blanks, and then ignores the trailing blanks when comparing two character strings. The second statement, however, generates trailing blanks inside a set of double quotation marks . Next, the statement compares the full set of characters on the left (including the quotation marks and the trailing blanks) to the full set of characters on the right. The two character strings are no longer equal.

How did the trailing blanks become part of the value of &CITY to begin with? Here is one unlikely possibility:

```
%LET CITY = %STR(NEW YORK    );
```

More likely, CALL SYMPUT copied the value of a DATA step variable, including trailing blanks:

```
IF      STATE = 'CA' THEN CITYNAME = 'SAN FRANCISCO';
ELSE IF STATE = 'NY' THEN CITYNAME = 'NEW YORK';
CALL SYMPUT('CITY', CITYNAME);
```

Instead, the program should have removed any trailing blanks:

```
CALL SYMPUT('CITY', TRIM(CITYNAME));
```

PROBLEM 44

Thinking Caps On

What does GRADE contain?

```
DATA SCHOOL;
DO STUDENT = 1 TO 10;
    OUTPUT;
END;

DATA GRADE;
DO UNTIL (DUMMY > 7);
    SET SCHOOL;
    DUMMY + 1;
END;
_N_ + 1;
OBSNO = _N_;
```

Tools and concepts:

DATA step flow
DO loops

```
DATA SCHOOL;
DO STUDENT = 1 TO 10;
   OUTPUT;
END;

DATA GRADE;
DO UNTIL (DUMMY > 7);
   SET SCHOOL;
   DUMMY + 1;
END;
_N_ + 1;
OBSNO = _N_;
```

First, consider _N_. What does it mean? What happens when you try to assign it a new value? The following basic principles apply:

- _N_ counts the number of times the program has left the DATA statement (not the number of observations read from SCHOOL). The program begins by leaving the DATA statement for the first time, and reading eight observations from SCHOOL in the DO loop. For that entire process, _N_=1.

- Assignment statements can reset the value of _N_; however, the reset is temporary. When the program leaves the DATA statement for the second time, _N_=2.

- _N_ always gets dropped from the final data set.

GRADE contains the following information:

STUDENT	DUMMY	OBSNO
8	8	2
9	9	3
10	10	4

The DO UNTIL loop performs the programming statements in the loop at least once, whether or not DUMMY > 7. The DO UNTIL condition gets checked at the END statement. The SET statement tracks which observations have been read and always reads the next observation. Because of these two factors, when the program leaves the DATA statement the second time, it enters the DO loop and reads the ninth observation from SCHOOL.

A Major League Problem

Raw data contain one line per city, along with the city's major league sports teams. City and team names may contain embedded blanks; however, each data value is separated from the next by two or more blanks. Using a single DATA step, create a SAS data set with CITY and the total number of teams in that CITY (one observation per CITY). The maximum length of a city name is 16 characters. Here are sample raw data:

```
SAN FRANCISCO      GIANTS    FORTYNINERS
LOS ANGELES    RAMS   RAIDERS   LAKERS       DODGERS
BOSTON    CELTICS      BRUINS    RED SOX
CHICAGO    CUBS    BULLS    WHITE SOX    BEARS    BLACKHAWKS
CHEYENNE
NEW YORK    YANKEES           METS   RANGERS    KNICKS
TORONTO               MAPLE LEAFS      BLUE JAYS
```

DO loops
Reading raw data

```
SAN FRANCISCO      GIANTS    FORTYNINERS
LOS ANGELES    RAMS  RAIDERS  LAKERS      DODGERS
BOSTON    CELTICS      BRUINS    RED SOX
CHICAGO    CUBS   BULLS    WHITE SOX    BEARS  BLACKHAWKS
CHEYENNE
NEW YORK   YANKEES          METS  RANGERS    KNICKS
TORONTO            MAPLE LEAFS      BLUE JAYS
```

Consider these three key tools for reading these raw data:

1. & on the INPUT statement scans from left to right, stopping when the program encounters the end of the data line or two blanks in a row.

2. MISSOVER on the INFILE statement gives a variable a missing value when attempting to read past the end of the line of raw data.

3. A trailing @ on the INPUT statement holds the same line of data for another INPUT statement. (Passing through the DATA statement also releases a data line held by a trailing @.)

Here's a program that uses these tools to read the data. For a city with four teams, the DO loop iterates five times:

```
DATA TEAMS;
INFILE RAWDATA MISSOVER;
LENGTH CITY $ 16;
INPUT CITY & $ @;
NTEAMS = -1;
DO UNTIL (TEAM=' ');
   INPUT TEAM & $ @;
   NTEAMS + 1;
END;
DROP TEAM;
```

In this case, the program drops TEAM. If it were being kept, however, it would have been defined as one character long by the DO statement. Although the subsequent INPUT statement reads more than one character, there would only be room to store the first of those characters in the variable TEAM. Regardless of the length of TEAM, it always has a missing value at the end of each observation.

PROBLEM 46

Do I Start to Date?

What is the final value of TOTAL?

```
DATA _NULL_;
RETAIN DATE '05JAN1960'D START 1;
DO I = START TO DATE;
   START = 3;
   DATE = 8;
   TOTAL = TOTAL + I + 1;
END;
TOTAL + I;
```

Tools and concepts:

Dates
DO loops
RETAIN statement/Sum statement

```
DATA _NULL_;
RETAIN DATE '05JAN1960'D START 1;
DO I = START TO DATE;
   START = 3;
   DATE = 8;
   TOTAL = TOTAL + I + 1;
END;
TOTAL + I;
```

The final value of TOTAL is 19. Four factors help bring about this result:

1. The initial value of DATE is 4 (not 5), since January 1, 1960, is day 0.

2. Because of the last statement, TOTAL is initially 0 and is retained. Even though the program mentions TOTAL in an earlier statement, these characteristics do not change.

3. The action of the DO loop is controlled by the initial values of START and DATE. Assignment statements inside the loop can change their values, but this has no effect on the action of the loop.

4. The DO loop increments I at the END statement, and then compares I to the upper limit of 4 (the initial value of DATE). Once I exceeds 4, the loop ends.

At these points, the factors above affect critical variables:

Point in Program	I	TOTAL
At beginning of DO loop	1	0
After TOTAL=	1	2
End of 1st iteration	2	2
After TOTAL=	2	5
End of 2nd iteration	3	5
After TOTAL=	3	9
End of 3rd iteration	4	9
After TOTAL=	4	14
End of 4th iteration	5	14
After final statement	5	19

What's That Number Again?

PROC PRINT on the data set ALLNAMES displayed Alice's phone number correctly, but it displayed Bob's phone number as (617) 938-0304. What happened?

```
DATA NEWNAMES;
INPUT NAME $ PHONE;
CARDS;
ALICE   5551234
BOB     6179380307
;

PROC FORMAT;
PICTURE PHONE           1000000-9999999='999-9999'
1000000000-9999999999=' 999) 999-9999' PREFIX='(';

DATA ALLNAMES;
UPDATE ALLNAMES NEWNAMES;
BY NAME;
FORMAT PHONE PHONE.;
```

Formats
Lengths of variables

```
DATA NEWNAMES;
INPUT NAME $ PHONE;
CARDS;
ALICE   5551234
BOB     6179380307
;

PROC FORMAT;
PICTURE PHONE          1000000-9999999='999-9999'
1000000000-9999999999=' 999) 999-9999' PREFIX='(';

DATA ALLNAMES;
UPDATE ALLNAMES NEWNAMES;
BY NAME;
FORMAT PHONE PHONE.;
```

The original data set ALLNAMES contained PHONE with a length of 5. When the UPDATE statement encountered ALLNAMES first, the SAS System assigned PHONE a length of 5 in the new data set. The length is too short to hold the full value of a ten-digit phone number.

If you test this sort of program, note that the maximum integer value that can be accurately stored varies not only with the length of the variable, but also with the operating system. Be prepared to see some variation in your results compared to those described here.

All Play and No Work

AGEDATA contains one observation and four variables:

```
NAME    AGE    BIRTH_D    BIRTH_M

JUDY    38       2          4
```

VACATION contains four observations and four variables:

```
NAME    LOCATION     DATE       BOOKED

JUDY    ARUBA       03/20/92   02/05/92
JUDY    BERMUDA     08/25/92   06/24/92
JUDY    CATSKILLS   05/05/92   04/01/92
JUDY    FLORIDA     02/12/92   01/30/92
```

What does this merge produce? (Assume that all dates are stored as unformatted SAS dates.)

```
DATA COMBINED (DROP=BIRTH_D BIRTH_M);
MERGE AGEDATA VACATION (DROP=DATE RENAME=(BOOKED=DATE));
BY NAME;
IF AGE = 38 AND NAME = 'JUDY' AND
DATE >= MDY(BIRTH_M,BIRTH_D,1992) THEN AGE = 39;
```

Tools and concepts:

Data set options
MERGE statement

The real issue here is that the variable names and values are stored in memory as opposed to the values in the incoming data sets. Let's follow the merge process with these guidelines in mind:

- DROP=DATE means that the variable DATE never gets read in from the VACATION data set.

- RENAME=(BOOKED=DATE) means that a variable called DATE exists in memory. Its value is obtained by reading the existing variable BOOKED.

- Since AGE comes from the "one" data set in a many-to-one merge, its value gets read in once and retained. AGE gets replicated on the various VACA-TION observations because it is retained, not because it is reread.

These are the values of the variables in memory at key points in the DATA step. (BIRTH_M is always 4, and BIRTH_D is always 2. Both get stored in memory, but dropped from the COMBINED data set.)

POINT	NAME	AGE	DATE	LOCATION
1st merge	JUDY	38	02/05/92	ARUBA
IF/THEN	JUDY	38	02/05/92	ARUBA
2nd merge	JUDY	38	06/24/92	BERMUDA
IF/THEN	JUDY	39	06/24/92	BERMUDA
3rd merge	JUDY	39	04/01/92	CATSKILLS
IF/THEN	JUDY	39	04/01/92	CATSKILLS
4th merge	JUDY	39	01/30/92	FLORIDA
IF/THEN	JUDY	39	01/30/92	FLORIDA

The final data set contains four observations, one for each location. NAME is always JUDY. AGE is 39 from the second observation onward. Once changed, it remains changed. DATE contains the values of the original BOOKED variable.

Why Me?

Describe the output, if any. If none, describe the outcome.

```
DATA BECAUSE;
DO Y = 1 TO 3;
    DO ME = 30 TO 50 BY 10;
        DO Y = 5 TO 8;
            DO ME = 41 TO 43;
                OUTPUT;
            END;
        END;
    END;
END;

PROC FREQ DATA=BECAUSE;
TABLES Y ME;
```

Tools and concepts:

DO loops

```
DATA BECAUSE;
DO Y = 1 TO 3;
    DO ME = 30 TO 50 BY 10;
        DO Y = 5 TO 8;
            DO ME = 41 TO 43;
                OUTPUT;
            END;
        END;
    END;
END;

PROC FREQ DATA=BECAUSE;
TABLES Y ME;
```

At each END statement, the corresponding variable (Y or ME) gets incremented by the BY amount for that DO loop. Once the variable exceeds the upper limit of the loop, that loop ends.

Here are the steps:

1. Give Y a value of 1 (first DO).

2. Give ME a value of 30 (second DO).

3. Change Y to 5 (third DO).

4. Change ME to 41 (fourth DO).

5. Continue through the innermost loop a total of three times (ME=41 TO 43), each time outputting an observation. At the end of the third iteration, increase ME from 43 to 44. That's when the innermost loop ends.

6. Repeat steps 4 and 5 with Y equal to 6, 7, and 8. A total of 12 observations get output, consisting of 4 for each ME value (41 to 43) and 3 for each Y value (5 to 8). At this point, the two innermost loops are over, ME is 44, and Y is 9.

7. At the third END statement, increase ME from 44 to 54. The second loop now ends, since 54 is greater than 50.

8. At the fourth END statement, increase Y from 9 to 10. The first loop now ends, since 10 is greater than 3.

I wouldn't recommend programming this way, but it is a "legal" program. If you do experiment with this program, be careful not to code an endless loop.

PROBLEM 50

To the End of the Line

The SAS data set XRAYS contains the variables X1-X9. Write a DATA step to realign the data values, pushing missing values to the higher-numbered variables. Here is a sample observation:

	X1	X2	X3	X4	X5	X6	X7	X8	X9
Initial values	.	.	4	.	2	.	.	5	.
Final values	4	2	5	.	.	.	.	.	.

Assume that there are no special missing numeric values such as .A or .B.

Tools and concepts:

    Arrays

    DO loops

Here's one program that pushes over the data values:

```
DATA XRAYS;
SET XRAYS;
ARRAY XXX {9} X1-X9;
I = 0;
DO J = 1 TO 9;
   IF XXX{J} > . THEN DO;
      I + 1;
      IF I < J THEN DO;
         XXX{I} = XXX{J};
         XXX{J} = .;
      END;
   END;
END;
```

As long as I = J, the DO loop has found only valid (nonmissing) values, and, therefore, it leaves the data unchanged. Once I < J, the DO loop has found at least one missing value, and, therefore, it swaps the variables. You can also "float" the nonmissing values to the left, by swapping missing values with adjacent nonmissing values:

```
DATA XRAYS;
SET XRAYS;
ARRAY XXX {9} X1-X9;
DO UNTIL (CHANGES=0);
   CHANGES = 0;
   DO I = 1 TO 8;
      IF XXX{I} = . AND XXX{I+1} > . THEN DO;
      CHANGES + 1;
      XXX{I} = XXX{I+1};
      XXX{I+1} = .;
   END;
END;
```

The second program probably takes longer to run.

PROBLEM 51

What's in a Name?

This program produced unusual output but no error messages. The title indicated there were 20 names, but the PROC FREQ table contained one output line, where all the names had missing values. What happened?

```
DATA _NULL_;
SET ALLDATA END=EOF;
BY NAME;
IF LAST.NAME;
COUNT + 1;
IF EOF THEN CALL SYMPUT('N', COMPRESS(COUNT));

PROC FREQ DATA=ALLDATA;
TABLES NAME / MISSING;
TITLE "COUNTS FOR ALL &N NAMES";
```

Tools and concepts:

PROC FREQ
Macro language

A few possibilities exist. Most likely, NAME is a character variable containing leading blanks. Since PROC FREQ operates on the first 16 characters of incoming variables, PROC FREQ would take different actual values of NAME to be missing if they started with 16 blanks.

Formats introduce another possibility:

```
PROC FORMAT;
VALUE $M LOW-HIGH = 'WHATEVER';

DATA ALLDATA;
SET ALLDATA;
FORMAT NAME $M.;

PROC FREQ DATA=ALLDATA;
TABLES NAME / MISSING;
```

When a format is in effect, PROC FREQ produces one row in the table for each formatted value of NAME. The format above groups all values of NAME into one formatted value. By default, PROC FORMAT tabulates the frequency count for each row using the lowest actual value encountered within each formatted range. If even one observation has a missing value for NAME, PROC FREQ stores the count for the only row in the table as a count of missing values (the lowest value in the format range).

One more possibility exists if NAME happens to be a numeric variable. Numeric variables can take on 28 unique values, all of which would be considered missing by PROC FREQ. Besides the usual missing value, 27 special missing values exist (._ and .A through .Z). The DATA step would consider each of these values to be different, but PROC FREQ would consider all of them to be missing.

No Men for All Ages

The log from this program reveals that MALES contains 200 observations, but BYAGE contains 0. There are no warning or error messages of any kind. What is/are the mystery statement(s)?

```
*MYSTERY STATEMENT(S);

DATA MALES;
SET ALL;
IF SEX = 'M';
TOTCOST = PRICE * QUANTITY;

PROC SORT DATA=MALES OUT=BYAGE;
BY AGE;
```

Tools and concepts:

      ???

The full program:

```
OPTIONS FIRSTOBS=201;

DATA MALES;
SET ALL;
IF SEX = 'M';
TOTCOST = PRICE * QUANTITY;

PROC SORT DATA=MALES OUT=BYAGE;
BY AGE;
```

The FIRSTOBS= option affects any subsequent step that reads data. In the case of the DATA step, it causes the SET statement to begin reading data with the 201st observation from ALL. The number of observations in ALL is unknown. Evidently, though, there were at least 400 observations to begin with. From the 201st observation onward, there were 200 that met the condition SEX='M'.

The FIRSTOBS option remains in effect as PROC SORT executes. Sorting reads in the observations, sorts them, and then writes them back out again. In this case, FIRSTOBS causes PROC SORT to begin reading the 201st observation from MALES. Since MALES contains only 200 observations, there are no observations in BYAGE.

Technically, the value of FIRSTOBS could have been any number greater than 200. Whatever the actual number, ALL would have to contain 200 observations with SEX='M' in the last portion of the data set.

Finally, note that the program must use IF, not WHERE, to subset observations. Current releases of the software do not permit a WHERE statement when the FIRSTOBS or OBS option limits the incoming observations.

The appendix lists this problem under "Global options."

PROBLEM 53

Lagging and Old Age

Rewrite this program so that you eliminate the LAG function but still get the same values for OLDAGE.

```
DATA NEW;
SET OLD;
IF NAME = 'BOB' THEN OLDAGE = LAG2(AGE);
```

Tools and concepts:

DATA step flow
Data set options
Functions
RETAIN statement/Sum statement

```
DATA NEW;
SET OLD;
IF NAME = 'BOB' THEN OLDAGE = LAG2(AGE);·
```

LAG2 retrieves the value of AGE from the second observation back that had the name of BOB (not the second observation back from OLD). One approach relies on the fact that each SET statement acts independently of other SET statements:

```
DATA NEW;
SET OLD;
IF NAME = 'BOB' THEN DO;
    N + 1;
    IF N > 2 THEN SET OLD (WHERE=(NAME='BOB')
            KEEP=NAME AGE RENAME=(AGE=OLDAGE));
END;
ELSE OLDAGE = .;
```

The last statement circumvents the problem that is caused by automatically retaining SET statement variables. Without the last statement, OLDAGE would have repeated for subsequent observations.

Another approach creates new variables instead of reading the data set twice with a second SET statement. For example:

```
DATA NEW;
SET OLD;
IF NAME = 'BOB' THEN DO;
    OLDAGE = BACK2;
    BACK2 = BACK1;
    BACK1 = AGE;
END;
RETAIN BACK1 BACK2;
DROP BACK1 BACK2;
```

This program works as long as AGE is a numeric variable. However, if AGE could be character, the program must define BACK1 and BACK2 as character with the same length as AGE. The following DO group would work. (The most efficient placement of this DO loop would be nested, immediately following the existing IF/THEN statement.)

```
IF 0 THEN DO;
   BACK1 = AGE;
   BACK2 = AGE;
END;
```

Since 0 is false, these assignment statements never execute. However, they affect the DATA step during compilation, defining the attributes of BACK1 and BACK2 based on AGE.

PROBLEM 54

Where Am I?

The following code attempted to set every numeric variable to 10 except for ID. In addition to ID, however, the 10th numeric variable (by position) remained unchanged. How could this have happened?

```
DATA NEW;
LENGTH ID 8;
SET OLD;
ARRAY NUMS {*} _NUMERIC_;
DO I = 2 TO DIM(NUMS)
    NUMS{I} = 10;
END;
```

Tools and concepts:

    Arrays

    DO loops

    Variable lists

```
DATA NEW;
LENGTH ID 8;
SET OLD;
ARRAY NUMS {*} _NUMERIC_;
DO I = 2 TO DIM(NUMS)
   NUMS{I} = 10;
END;
```

The original data set OLD contains the numeric variable I. Therefore, I is part of the NUMS array. For the 10th variable to remain unchanged, I must be the 9th numeric variable. When the DO loop executes with I=9, it changes I to 10. At the END statement, I gets increased to 11; so, the DO loop never executes with I=10, and the 10th numeric variable remains unchanged.

This program illustrates the following two dangers of leaving stray variables named I (or N or DUMMY or COUNT, select your favorite):

1. The program, as it stands, generates no warning or error messages. It leaves one of the variables unchanged without notifying the programmer. If I were the 5th variable instead of the 9th, the program would leave five variables unchanged without warning.

2. If I were the 11th (or higher) numeric variable, the program would contain an endless loop. This situation would occur any time the value being assigned in the loop (in this case, 10) was less than the position of I in the array.

As Easy As ABC

Under what conditions do these statements produce identical results?

```
IF A = 1 AND B = 2 OR C = 3 THEN DELETE;
IF A = 1 THEN IF B = 2 OR C = 3 THEN DELETE;
```

Tools and concepts:

None

```
IF A = 1 AND B = 2 OR C = 3 THEN DELETE;
IF A = 1 THEN IF B = 2 OR C = 3 THEN DELETE;
```

Since AND gets evaluated before OR, the first statement is equivalent to:

```
IF (A = 1 AND B = 2) OR C = 3 THEN DELETE;
```

The easiest way to compare these statements is to list all the cases.

A	B	C	Statement 1		Statement 2
0	0	0	False	=	False
0	0	3	True		False
0	2	0	False	=	False
0	2	3	True		False
1	0	0	False	=	False
1	0	3	True	=	True
1	2	0	True	=	True
1	2	3	True	=	True

Of course, values of 0 in this listing represent any nonmatching value (A not 1, B not 2, or C not 3).

Most of the time both statements produce the same result. The only differences occur when

A=1 is false, and

C=3 is true.

PROBLEM 56

Five Brides, One Wedding

The following program produced an unusual result. Although the data set BRIDES contained five observations, the data set WEDDINGS contained only one observation. How could this have happened?

```
OPTIONS OBS=MAX;


DATA WEDDINGS;
MERGE BRIDES (IN=INLOVE) GROOMS;
BY CHAPLAIN;
IF INLOVE;
```

Tools and concepts:

Data set options
MERGE statement

```
OPTIONS OBS=MAX;


DATA WEDDINGS;
MERGE BRIDES (IN=INLOVE) GROOMS;
BY CHAPLAIN;
IF INLOVE;
```

The GROOMS data set contains the variable INLOVE. MERGE assigns INLOVE a value of 1 when reading an observation from BRIDES. However, when MERGE proceeds to read an observation from GROOMS, it overwrites INLOVE. These data sets could have produced the result:

BRIDES	GROOMS	
CHAPLAIN	CHAPLAIN	INLOVE
A	A	0
B	B	0
C	C	0
D	D	5
E	E	0

After the MERGE, only the fourth observation remains. The software interprets 0 as false and 5 as true.

PROBLEM 57

Close, But No Cigar

The data set OLD contains only the numeric variable CIGAR, which never has a missing value. Write a single DATA step to add a second variable CLOSE. For each observation, examine the values of CIGAR on every other observation. Assign to CLOSE the numerically closest CIGAR from another observation. OLD is not in sorted order. For example:

CIGAR	CLOSE
8	8
3	2
8	8
1	2
2	1 or 3 (take your pick)
12	8

Tools and concepts:

Arrays
DATA step flow
Data set options
Macro language
RETAIN statement/Sum statement
SET statement options

To find CLOSE in a single DATA step:

```
DATA CLOSEST (DROP=I TEST);
SET OLD NOBS=TOTALOBS;
DO I = 1 TO TOTALOBS;
   IF _N_ NE I THEN DO;
      SET OLD (RENAME=(CIGAR=TEST)) POINT=I;
      IF CLOSE = . THEN CLOSE = TEST;
      ELSE IF ABS(CIGAR - CLOSE) >
               ABS(CIGAR - TEST)
      THEN CLOSE = TEST;
   END;
END;
```

The first SET statement reads observations sequentially. For each observation, the second SET uses the POINT= option to read every other observation, enabling numeric comparisons to be made. When _N_= I, it means that both SET statements would be reading the same observation.

While this program works, it is quite expensive. If the OLD data set contains 10,000 observations, the DO loop reads the entire data set 10,000 times (using POINT= every time)! It would be more efficient to sort the data set first and use a two-step solution. For example:

```
PROC SORT DATA=OLD;
BY CIGAR;

DATA CLOSEST (DROP=PREVIOUS NEXT);
SET OLD END=EOF;
PREVIOUS = LAG(CIGAR);
IF NOT EOF THEN SET OLD
(RENAME=(CIGAR=NEXT) FIRSTOBS=2);
ELSE DO;
   CLOSE = PREVIOUS;
   RETURN;
END;
```

```
IF .< ABS(CIGAR - PREVIOUS) <
    ABS(CIGAR - NEXT)
THEN CLOSE = PREVIOUS;
ELSE CLOSE = NEXT;
```

Because of the sorted order of the data, this program reads OLD only twice. The first SET statement retrieves the current value of CIGAR. The LAG function retrieves the value on the previous observation. Finally, the second SET statement retrieves the value on the next observation.

The major drawback of the second program is that it does not apply to real-life situations. This problem is really a simplification. Typical "closest match" problems base the match on a combination of variables, rather than on a single variable. There is no sorted order that does the job when the formula for closeness is

```
(X - x)**2 + (Y - y)**2
```

where X and Y are the values on the current observation, and x and y are values from another observation.

Finally, if your machine has enough memory, converting the observations to variables may be fastest. Run through all the variables in memory to make the comparisons. For example:

```
DATA _NULL_;
CALL SYMPUT('N', PUT(TOTOBS, 5.));
STOP;
SET OLD NOBS=TOTOBS;

DATA CLOSEST (KEEP=CLOSE CIGAR);
ARRAY VAL {&N};
DO I = 1 TO &N;
    SET OLD;
    VAL{I} = CIGAR;
END;
```

```
DO I = 1 TO &N;
   CIGAR = VAL{I};
   CLOSE = .;
   DO J = 1 TO &N;
      IF I NE J THEN DO;
         IF CLOSE = . THEN CLOSE = VAL{J};
         ELSE IF ABS(CIGAR - CLOSE) >
                  ABS(CIGAR - VAL{J})
         THEN CLOSE = VAL{J};
      END;
   END;
   OUTPUT;
END;
STOP;
```

The first DATA step assigns the number of observations in OLD to a macro variable. This represents the number of variables that the second DATA step must create. Given sufficient memory to hold the variables, the second DATA step (top half) reads in the original data and converts the observations to variables and then (bottom half) makes the comparisons. By creating a second array, this program could create two sets of variables and could make the comparisons based on two variables instead of one. The efficiency tradeoff: the program runs faster but requires more memory and is more complex.

PROBLEM 58

Reading and 'Rriting and 'Rithmetic

What is the final value of N? Assume that TEMP.SAS already exists but is empty before
the DATA step begins.

```
DATA FINAL;
N = 2;
FILE 'TEMP.SAS' NOPRINT;
PUT 'DO I = 1 TO 5 BY 4;';
PUT 'END;';
%INCLUDE 'TEMP.SAS';
N = N + I;
```

Tools and concepts:

DATA step flow
DO loops

```
DATA FINAL;
N = 2;
FILE 'TEMP.SAS' NOPRINT;
PUT 'DO I = 1 TO 5 BY 4;';
PUT 'END;';
%INCLUDE 'TEMP.SAS';
N = N + I;
```

The final value of N is a missing value.

This problem is based on two key features:

1. TEMP.SAS is empty before the DATA step begins.

2. The %INCLUDE statement has its effect as the DATA step is compiled, before executing the FILE and PUT statements.

As a result, the %INCLUDE statement brings in an empty data set, adding zero lines of code to the program. The DATA step executes as if the %INCLUDE statement were not even there. Therefore, the variable I is missing, and the final assignment statement generates a missing value for N.

If the DATA step ran twice in a row, the results of the second DATA step would be different. The first DATA step would write two lines to TEMP.SAS, and the second DATA step would find those lines with the %INCLUDE statement. The following DATA step would generate a final value of 11 for the variable N:

```
DATA FINAL;
N = 2;
DO I = 1 TO 5 BY 4;
END;
N = N + I;
```

The DO loop doesn't end until I exceeds the upper limit of 5. This requires a total of two iterations through the loop, each increasing I by 4.

PROBLEM 59

Numbers Games

What are the values of GAME1, GAME2, GAME3, and GAME4?

```
DATA NUMBERS;
ORIGINAL = 1234;
GAME1 = INPUT(ORIGINAL, 4.);
GAME2 = INPUT(ORIGINAL, 7.1);
GAME3 = INPUT(ORIGINAL, 10.2);
GAME4 = INPUT(ORIGINAL, 13.3);
```

Tools and concepts:

Functions

```
DATA NUMBERS;
ORIGINAL = 1234;
GAME1 = INPUT(ORIGINAL, 4.);
GAME2 = INPUT(ORIGINAL, 7.1);
GAME3 = INPUT(ORIGINAL, 10.2);
GAME4 = INPUT(ORIGINAL, 13.3);
```

The INPUT function requires a character string as the first parameter. Since ORIGINAL is a numeric variable, the INPUT function converts it to a character string. By default, numeric-to-character conversions use the BEST12. format; therefore, all four INPUT functions read a character string consisting of eight blanks followed by the digits 1234.

What does an informat of 13.3 mean? The width (13) means "read 13 characters of the incoming character string." The decimal place (.3) means "inspect those 13 characters to see if they contain a decimal point." If they do, that's where the decimal point belongs. If they don't, assume the last three digits read fall after the decimal point. In this problem, the incoming character string never contains a decimal point.

Here are the values for GAME1, GAME2, GAME3, and GAME4:

GAME1=.
The INPUT function reads four characters from the incoming character string. Since all four characters are blank, the value for GAME1 is missing.

GAME2=.
The INPUT function reads seven characters from the incoming character string. Again, all the characters are blank.

GAME3=0.12
The INPUT function reads 10 characters, consisting of eight blanks plus the digits 12. Since the INPUT function found no decimal point, the 10.2 informat assumes that the last two digits fall after the decimal point.

GAME4=1.234
The INPUT function reads all 12 characters (there is no 13th character). Since the INPUT function again found no decimal point, the 13.3 informat assumes that the last three digits fall after the decimal point.

PROBLEM 60

Isolate the Troublemakers

When these data sets are merged by NAME, a note appears stating:

> MERGE STATEMENT HAS MORE THAN ONE DATA SET WITH REPEATS
> OF BY VALUES.

Although the combination of AMY and BOB would generate this note, CHUCK is commonly the true troublemaker. Modify the DATA step below so it prints a message about CHUCK (and all like him), but not about AMY or BOB.

```
GOAL DATA SET           REWARD DATA SET


NAME   DEGREE           NAME   LOCATION


AMY    B.S.             AMY    ARUBA
BOB    B.S.             AMY    ANTWERP
BOB    M.S.             AMY    ARGENTINA
BOB    Ph.D.            BOB    BERMUDA
CHUCK  B.S.             CHUCK  CANCUN
CHUCK  M.S.             CHUCK  CARACAS
CHUCK  Ph.D.
```

```
DATA BOTH;
MERGE GOAL REWARD;
BY NAME;
```

Tools and concepts:

Data set options
MERGE statement

```
DATA BOTH;
MERGE GOAL (IN=G) REWARD (IN=R);
BY NAME;
```

The IN= variables (G and R) tell you whether an observation came (in part) from a particular data set. MERGE assigns values to IN= variables at two points:

1. when beginning a new BY group, MERGE sets all IN= variables to 0.

2. when reading an observation, MERGE sets the IN= variable for that source of data to 1.

A program can assign different values to IN= variables and can expect the MERGE statement to replace those values at the two points described above:

```
DATA BOTH;
G = 5;
R = 5;
MERGE GOAL (IN=G) REWARD (IN=R);
BY NAME;
```

Now G and R are 1 for the first observation for each name. Except for the troublemakers, either G or R become 5 for all subsequent observations for a name. The program can easily spot the troublemakers: observations with FIRST.NAME equal to 0, and with G and R both equal to 1.

```
DATA BOTH;
G = 5;
R = 5;
MERGE GOAL (IN=G) REWARD (IN=R);
BY NAME;
IF FIRST.NAME THEN N = 1;
ELSE DO;
   N + 1;
   IF N = 2 AND G = 1 AND R = 1 THEN PUT
   NAME 'IS A TROUBLEMAKER.';
END;
```

PROBLEM 61

How Much Is Half?

Sketch the final data set.

```
DATA INCOMING;
DO I = 3 TO 10;
   HALF = 3 - FLOOR(-I/2);
   OUTPUT;
END;

DATA OUTGOING;
DO HALF = 3 TO 8;
   SET INCOMING POINT=HALF;
   OUTPUT;
END;
STOP;
```

Tools and concepts:

    DATA step flow

    Functions

    SET statement options

```
DATA INCOMING;
DO I = 3 TO 10;
   HALF = 3 - FLOOR(-I/2);
   OUTPUT;
END;

DATA OUTGOING;
DO HALF = 3 TO 8;
   SET INCOMING POINT=HALF;
   OUTPUT;
END;
STOP;
```

When the FLOOR function receives a non-integer argument, it returns the next lowest integer. Thus INCOMING contains:

I	HALF		
3	5		
4	5		
5	6	→	output I to OUTGOING
6	6		
7	7		
8	7		
9	8	→	output I to OUTGOING
10	8		

The variable HALF performs triple duty in the final DATA step: it controls the DO loop, it is the POINT= variable (and therefore gets dropped from OUTGOING), and it is read in by the SET statement. So the final DATA step

1. reads in the third observation (I=5, HALF=6), and outputs I.

2. increases HALF from 6 to 7 at the END statement.

3. reads in the seventh observation (I=9, HALF=8), and outputs I.

4. increases HALF from 8 to 9 at the END statement. Since the outer bound of the DO loop is 8, the loop now ends.

5. executes the STOP statement, halting the DATA step.

PROBLEM 62

The Case of the Disappearing Semicolons

The following code contains eight statements. What is the smallest number of statements that produces the same values for STATUS?

```
SCORE = 100;
IF DRINKER  = 'Y' THEN SCORE = SCORE - 10;
IF SMOKER   = 'Y' THEN SCORE = SCORE - 20;
IF NIGHTOWL = 'Y' THEN SCORE = SCORE -  5;
IF EXERCISE = 'Y' THEN SCORE = SCORE + 30;
IF      SCORE <= 70 THEN STATUS = 1;
ELSE IF SCORE < 100 THEN STATUS = 2;
ELSE                     STATUS = 3;
```

Tools and concepts:

Logical comparisons

```
SCORE = 100;
IF DRINKER  = 'Y' THEN SCORE = SCORE - 10;
IF SMOKER   = 'Y' THEN SCORE = SCORE - 20;
IF NIGHTOWL = 'Y' THEN SCORE = SCORE -  5;
IF EXERCISE = 'Y' THEN SCORE = SCORE + 30;
IF      SCORE <= 70 THEN STATUS = 1;
ELSE IF SCORE < 100 THEN STATUS = 2;
ELSE                     STATUS = 3;
```

Logical comparisons can easily replace the computation of SCORE and STATUS with a single statement apiece. The SAS System automatically replaces each logical comparison with a 1 (if true) or a 0 (if false):

```
SCORE = 100 - 10 * (DRINKER='Y')
            - 20 * (SMOKER='Y')
            -  5 * (NIGHTOWL='Y')
            + 30 * (EXERCISE='Y');
STATUS = 2 + (SCORE >= 100) - (SCORE <= 70);
```

A few variations exist for the second statement, such as the following:

```
STATUS = 1 + (SCORE > 70) + (SCORE >= 100);
STATUS = (SCORE <= 70) + 2 * (70 < SCORE < 100)
                       + 3 * (SCORE >= 100);
```

Once you've gotten this far, it is straightforward to replace the original code with a single statement:

```
STATUS = 2 + ( (100 - 10 * (DRINKER='Y')
                     - 20 * (SMOKER='Y')
                     -  5 * (NIGHTOWL='Y')
                     + 30 * (EXERCISE='Y'))
                >= 100)
          - ( (100 - 10 * (DRINKER='Y')
                     - 20 * (SMOKER='Y')
                     -  5 * (NIGHTOWL='Y')
                     + 30 * (EXERCISE='Y'))
                <= 70);
```

Personally, I wouldn't replace the code with a single statement in practice. One statement seems much more difficult to read compared to the original.

PROBLEM 63

A Hidden Flaw

What goes wrong with this multi-column report?

```
DATA _NULL_;
FILE PRINT PAGESIZE=60 N=PS NOTITLES
          LINESIZE=132;
PUT #1 @60 'FAVORITE NAMES';
DO COL = 1, 45, 89;
   DO LINE = 3 TO 60;
      SET ALLNAMES;
      PUT #LINE @COL NAME;
   END;
END;
PUT _PAGE_;
```

Tools and concepts:

Customized reporting

```
DATA _NULL_;
FILE PRINT PAGESIZE=60 N=PS NOTITLES
          LINESIZE=132;
PUT #1 @60 'FAVORITE NAMES';
DO COL = 1, 45, 89;
   DO LINE = 3 TO 60;
      SET ALLNAMES;
      PUT #LINE @COL NAME;
   END;
END;
PUT _PAGE_;
```

This is a standard form for a program that prints a telephone-book-style report: the first 56 observations in one column, the next 56 in a second column, and the next 56 in a third column. The problem arises when beginning a new column, for example when COL=45 and LINE=3. When the PUT statement begins, the SAS System notices that the last line written was line 60 (the last line on the page). Therefore, before repositioning to line 3 (#LINE), SAS ejects the current page and begins a new page. To work around this problem, add a trailing @ to the PUT statement as follows:

```
PUT #LINE @COL NAME @;
```

Now writing to the last line no longer causes a page eject. Each line, including the last, is held and is available for a subsequent PUT statement.

PROBLEM 64

Musical Chairs

When this program ran twice (against different data sets), the order of the STATE values changed. Both data sets had the same structure (same variable attributes), and any formats in effect were identical from one run to the next. What happened?

```
PROC MEANS DATA=USASALES SUM;
CLASS STATE;
VAR SALES;
```

STATE	SUM		STATE	SUM
VT	1000		MA	3000
NY	2000		VT	2000
MA	1500		NY	5000

Formats

PROC MEANS/PROC SUMMARY

```
PROC MEANS DATA=USASALES SUM;
CLASS STATE;
VAR SALES;
```

STATE	SUM		STATE	SUM
VT	1000		MA	3000
NY	2000		VT	2000
MA	1500		NY	5000

For the states to appear in unsorted order, the printed values must be formatted values rather than actual values of STATE. How could the same format print in more than one order? Here is one possibility:

```
PROC FORMAT;
VALUE STNAME  1, 101, 1001 = 'VT'
              2, 102, 1002 = 'NY'
              3, 103, 1003 = 'MA';


DATA USASALES;
SET USASALES;
FORMAT STATE STNAME.;
```

Now the order of the states depends on which values appear in the USASALES data set. The printed order is from the lowest to the highest actual (numeric) value of STATE.

Notice that the CLASS statement does not print a summary for the entire data set. If PROC MEANS produced an output data set, the data set would contain both levels of summarization. However, the printed output from PROC MEANS does not contain a summary line for all states combined.

PROBLEM 65

The Spirit of Giving

These programs actually produced different results. GIFT1 contained 5 observations, while GIFT2 contained just 1 observation. How could this have happened?

```
DATA GIFT1;                        DATA GIFT2;
MERGE FROMME                       MERGE TOYOU
(KEEP=FREEWILL IN=LOVE)            (KEEP=FREEWILL)
        TOYOU                              FROMME
(KEEP=FREEWILL);                   (KEEP=FREEWILL IN=LOVE);
BY FREEWILL;                       BY FREEWILL;
IF LOVE;                           IF LOVE;
```

Tools and concepts:

Lengths of variables

MERGE statement

```
DATA GIFT1;                    DATA GIFT2;
MERGE FROMME                   MERGE TOYOU
(KEEP=FREEWILL IN=LOVE)         (KEEP=FREEWILL)
       TOYOU                          FROMME
(KEEP=FREEWILL);               (KEEP=FREEWILL IN=LOVE);
BY FREEWILL;                   BY FREEWILL;
IF LOVE;                       IF LOVE;
```

It looks simple: this could never happen. Actually, the problem is that FREEWILL is a character variable with different lengths in the two incoming data sets. The program determines the length of FREEWILL from the first data set mentioned in the MERGE statement. It then merges the data sets based on the number of characters in the length of FREEWILL. These data sets could have produced the results described:

■ FREEWILL in FROMME has a length of 1:

```
B
```

■ FREEWILL in TOYOU has a length of 6:

```
B
BO
BOB
BOBBIE
BOBBY
```

The GIFT1 DATA step defines FREEWILL as one character long and matches from the two data sets based on the first character of FREEWILL. The GIFT2 DATA step defines FREEWILL as six characters long and, therefore, finds a match on only the first observation.

The Final Stages

What are the three final stages?

```
PROC FORMAT;
VALUE $RECODE   '10'='80'    '20'='10'    '30'='50'
                '40'='90'    '50'='110'   '60'='20'
                '70'='120'   '80'='30'    '90'='70'
                '100'='40'   '110'='100'  '120'='60';

DATA SCRAMBLE;
DO STAGE = '20', '50', '100';
   IF STAGE >= '100' THEN STAGE =
      PUT(PUT(STAGE, $RECODE.), $RECODE.);
   ELSE STAGE = PUT(STAGE, $RECODE.);
   OUTPUT;
END;
```

Functions
Lengths of variables

```
PROC FORMAT;
VALUE $RECODE   '10'='80'    '20'='10'    '30'='50'
                '40'='90'    '50'='110'   '60'='20'
                '70'='120'   '80'='30'    '90'='70'
                '100'='40'   '110'='100'  '120'='60';

DATA SCRAMBLE;
DO STAGE = '20', '50', '100';
   IF STAGE >= '100' THEN STAGE =
      PUT(PUT(STAGE, $RECODE.), $RECODE.);
   ELSE STAGE = PUT(STAGE, $RECODE.);
   OUTPUT;
END;
```

When comparing one character string to another, the SAS System compares from left to right, starting with the first character. As character strings, then, 20 > 100 since 2 > 1. Similarly, the second time through the loop, 50 > 100 since 5 > 1.

STAGE has a length of 2 since the first mention of STAGE sets it equal to '20'. As a result, when the IF/THEN statement compares STAGE (length of 2) to '100' (length of 3), it appends a blank as the third character of the shorter string.

The third time through the loop, STAGE has an initial value of '10', not '100'. As character strings, 10 < 100. Since both strings begin with the same two characters, the determination is made by comparing the third character of each string. Blank is less than 0, therefore 10 is less than 100. The results:

Observation	Incoming STAGE	Final STAGE
1	20	80
2	50	10
3	10	80

On the second observation, the innermost PUT function generates the characters '110'. Since that value is used as the argument to the outermost PUT function (rather than being assigned as the value of STRING), there is no reason to truncate '110' down to a length of 2.

Below Average Results

This program attempts to compute the average number of days between visits for each patient. Why won't the program work? Assume DATE is a SAS date.

```
DATA AVGDAYS;
N = 0;
DO UNTIL (LAST.PATIENT);
   SET VISITS;
   BY PATIENT DATE;
   IF FIRST.PATIENT THEN FIRSTDAY = DATE;
   N + 1;
END;
AVGDAYS = (DATE - FIRSTDAY) / N;
```

        DATA step flow
        Dates

```
DATA AVGDAYS;
N=0;
DO UNTIL (LAST.PATIENT);
   SET VISITS;
   BY PATIENT DATE;
   IF FIRST.PATIENT THEN FIRSTDAY = DATE;
   N + 1;
END;
AVGDAYS = (DATE - FIRSTDAY) / N;
```

The program contains the following good features:

■ The DO UNTIL loop reads through all observations for a given value of PATIENT.

■ The difference of DATE – FIRSTDAY is the proper numerator. Consider an alternative approach. For each observation, compute the difference between the previous DATE and the current DATE. Then average those differences. The difference of DATE – FIRSTDAY is the same as the sum of all the individual differences. The mathematics of it for a PATIENT with four observations are

$$A - D \ = \ (A - B) \ + \ (B - C) \ + \ (C - D)$$

■ The variable N accurately counts the number of observations for each PATIENT.

There's the error! With four observations, a PATIENT has only three values for "number of days between visits." The proper last statement should guard against division by zero:

```
IF N > 1 THEN
AVGDAYS = (DATE - FIRSTDAY) / (N - 1);
```

PROBLEM 68

Back to School

These two programs produced different results. JRHIGH1 contained 5 observations, while JRHIGH2 contained just 1 observation. How could this have happened?

```
DATA JRHIGH1;              DATA JRHIGH2;
MERGE GRADE8 GRADE9;       MERGE GRADE8 GRADE9;
BY STUDENT;                BY STUDENT;
WHERE GPA > 3;             IF GPA > 3;
```

Tools and concepts:

MERGE statement
Subsetting IF/DELETE
WHERE statement

```
DATA JRHIGH1;                    DATA JRHIGH2;
MERGE GRADE8 GRADE9;             MERGE GRADE8 GRADE9;
BY STUDENT;                      BY STUDENT;
WHERE GPA > 3;                   IF GPA > 3;
```

Since both programs produced an output data set, there must have been no error messages. As a result, GPA must appear in both GRADE8 and GRADE9. Otherwise the WHERE statement would have generated an error message.

Once you know that both data sets contain GPA, this becomes a merge problem. What combination of GPA values would produce different subsets? The answer relies on the fact that IF and WHERE subset differently. IF reads in every observation and then deletes those that are not needed. WHERE reads in only the needed observations. This is one possible version of the incoming data:

GRADE8			GRADE9	
STUDENT	GPA		STUDENT	GPA
AMY	4		AMY	2
BOB	4		BOB	3
CAROL	2		CAROL	1
DONALD	4		DONALD	5
EDWARD	5		EDWARD	3
FRANK	4		FRANK	2

Now the subsetting IF reads in all of the information and deletes all observations except DONALD. The WHERE statement reads in all observations where GPA > 3 and outputs all of them. Everyone except CAROL appears in the final data set.

Is It Safe to Come Out?

Raw data for toxic waste dumps contain estimated safety dates in columns 1 through 6. Column 1 indicates century (1=20th century, 2=21st century, through 9=28th century), while columns 2 through 6 contain a Julian date. For example, 193001 is January 1, 1993. 703026 is January 26, 2503. Assign SASDATE the proper SAS date value by completing the INPUT and assignment statements below:

```
DATA SAFEDATE;
INFILE TOXIC;
INPUT   ...  ;
SASDATE = ...  ;
```

Dates

Functions

Logical comparisons

Consider this initial program:

```
DATA SAFEDATE;
INFILE TOXIC;
INPUT  CENTURY 1. YEAR 2. DAY 3.;
SASDATE = DAY + MDY(12, 31, 1899 + YEAR +
                    100 * (CENTURY - 1) );
```

With known values for CENTURY and YEAR, the MDY function can compute the proper SAS date for December 31 of the preceding year. To complete the solution, just add in the number of days. This initial program comes up short in one respect. The following date

100001

represents January 1, 2000 since the year 2000 is part of the 20th century. However, the program computes the date as January 1, 1900. The program requires one final modification to compute dates accurately:

```
DATA SAFEDATE;
INFILE TOXIC;
INPUT  CENTURY 1. YEAR 2. DAY 3.;
SASDATE = DAY + MDY(12, 31, 1899 + YEAR +
                    100 * (CENTURY - 1 +
                    (YEAR=0)) );
```

Now the logical comparison YEAR=0 gets evaluated and replaced with 1 (if true) or 0 (if false). So if YEAR=0, the program adds 100 to the third argument in the MDY function.

Finally, the relatively new JULIANw. informats can handle a four-digit year. This alternative approach still requires that special attention be paid when YEAR=0. The following statement would convert 393001 to a Julian value of 2193001 as the first argument in the PUT function:

```
SASDATE = INPUT(PUT(DAY + YEAR * 1000 + 1800000 +
                    100000 * (CENTURY + (YEAR=0))),
              7.),
              JULIAN7.);
```

PROBLEM 70

Counting Calories

You just finished generating a table via a 101-line format:

```
PROC FORMAT;
VALUE TWENTY      0 = '    0'
                1-20 = '    1-  20'
               21-40 = '   21-  40'
                      . . .

           1981-2000 = '1981-2000';

PROC FREQ DATA=FOODS;
TABLES CALORIES;
FORMAT CALORIES TWENTY.;
```

Of course, your boss says, "This doesn't look quite right. Try it with groups of 25 instead of 20." Knowing that your boss is likely to change his or her mind again (and strangling the boss is not a viable option), rewrite the program to make your life easy. You may assume that (1) CALORIES takes on integer values only, (2) CALORIES ranges from 0 to a maximum of 2000, (3) the boss always wants equal size groups, and (4) the labeling style for a group must remain at least approximately the same as it is now (for example, 1–25 and   1 –   25 are both fine). Use of macro language is allowed, but not necessary.

Tools and concepts:

> DO loops
> Formats
> Macro language

Two methods can automate the creation of a format:

1. Store the needed information in a SAS data set, and use the CNTLIN= option on PROC FORMAT to construct a format based on that data set instead of a VALUE statement.

2. Use macro language to define the ranges in a VALUE statement.

The first method requires that a SAS data set contains the necessary information: the name of the format, the starting and ending points of each range, and the labels to assign to each range. PROC FORMAT expects that certain reserved variable names represent these pieces of information:

■ FMTNAME for the format name

■ START for the beginning of each range

■ END for the end of each range

■ LABEL for the label of each range.

If the wrong variable names have been used, it is easy to rename variables on the PROC statement. However, all variables must exist in the SAS data set. It's easy to forget to create a variable representing the name of the format. The following program could have created the original format (using groups of 20):

```
DATA TEMP;
FMTNAME = 'TWENTY';
GSIZE = 20;
START = 0;
END = 0;
LENGTH LABEL $ 9;
LABEL = '    0';
OUTPUT;
DO START = 1 TO 2000 BY GSIZE;
   END = START + GSIZE - 1;
   LABEL = PUT(START,4.) || '-' || PUT(END,4.);
   OUTPUT;
END;

PROC FORMAT CNTLIN=TEMP;
```

Creating GSIZE rather than hard coding the number 20 complicates the program slightly. However, changing only one spot in the program (the value of GSIZE) adjusts the size of the groupings.

Using macro language actually provides for a slightly shorter program:

```
%MACRO GROUP (GSIZE=);

    PROC FORMAT;
    VALUE TWENTY  0 = '    0'
    %DO I=1 %TO   2000 %BY &GSIZE;
       %LET J = %EVAL(&I + &GSIZE - 1);
       &I - &J = "&I - &J"
    %END;
    ;

%MEND GROUP;

%GROUP (GSIZE=20)
```

or

```
%GROUP (GSIZE=25)
```

Both programs continue to use a format name of TWENTY, regardless of the size of the groupings. That's easy enough to change.

The strange-looking portion of this program is the embedding of macro language statements within a SAS language statement. The VALUE statement begins with the keyword VALUE and ends with the semicolon beneath the keyword %END. In between, each macro language statement ends with a semicolon. The text

```
&I - &J = "&I - &J"
```

is not a macro language statement, and therefore does not end with a semicolon. Since it is not a macro language statement, those characters (after resolving for &I and &J) become the next words in the VALUE statement. Each line generated this way defines another range within the format. For example, the first such line contains

```
1 - 20 = "1 - 20"
```

APPENDIX

LIST OF PROBLEMS BY TOOLS AND CONCEPTS

The next few pages list the problem numbers according to the tools and concepts found in the solutions. If you find a problem difficult, use this list to locate additional problems on the same topic.

Within a single topic, all problems listed either require that topic to solve the problem or use that topic in an interesting, nontrivial way. Trivial use is omitted. For example, many problems contain a PUT statement but do not necessarily appear under "Customized reporting." On the other hand, a solution may demonstrate a related or incorrect program that uses a tool listed here. In that case, as long as the use is interesting or important, this appendix lists the problem under that topic.

These are problem numbers, not page numbers.

Arrays

10, 14, 16, 21, 39, 50, 54, 57

Comments

4, 17

Customized reporting

3, 5, 21, 63

DATA step flow

5, 9, 11, 12, 18, 20, 26, 28, 37, 42, 44, 53, 57, 58, 61, 67

Data set options

18, 23, 33, 48, 53, 56, 57, 60

Dates

46, 67, 69

Detecting end-of-file

12, 18, 24

DO loops

6, 10, 13, 14, 15, 16, 28, 44, 45, 46, 49, 50, 54, 58, 70